informed consent

James E. Ludlam

American Hospital Association
840 North Lake Shore Drive
Chicago, Illinois 60611

Library of Congress Cataloging in Publication Data

Ludlam, James E.

    Informed consent.

    Includes bibliographical references and index.
    1. Informed consent (Medical law)—United States.
I. Title.
KF3827.15L8   344'.73'041   78-24495
ISBN 0-87258-243-4

AHA catalog no. 1160

©1978 by the
American Hospital Association
840 North Lake Shore Drive
Chicago, Illinois 60611

Printed in the U.S.A.
12M-11/78-6449
8M-10/79-6903

contents

foreword

The matter of an informed consent is of immeasurable importance to the patient and to the attending physician. It is also important to the hospital, but the hospital's interest will reflect its desire to assist members of its medical staff in meeting their obligations to the patient and in protecting the patient's welfare, as well as the instances in which the physician may be considered a hospital employee in legal contemplation.

The issue of informed consent has tended to become surrounded by some mystique and uncertainty, due in part to the variety of judicial and statutory developments that have taken place among the states. Among the purposes of this book, commissioned by the American Hospital Association, are to bring more light to the subject by focusing on the underlying principles and rationale of informed consent and to identify the somewhat disparate paths the doctrine has taken at the hands of different courts and state legislatures. To assist our readers in researching their own state's law, a list of authorities cited, including cases, statutes, law reviews, and other references, has been provided. The author has also documented the judicial development of required consents, provided an overview of relevant state statutes, and suggested a model statute when a legislative approach is thought to be appropriate.

Because informed consent is a matter regulated by state law, it lacks uniformity. For this reason in particular, the study should be regarded as one for reference and general information only and not to be used for legal guidance. While this publication will provide a useful reference for attorneys for both the practical and legal considerations that relate to the doctrine, it is commended to all persons involved in the health care field, including particularly those who participate in developing legislative programs.

The author of the study is James E. Ludlam (B.A., Stanford University, 1936; J.D., Harvard Law School, 1939), an attorney who is both prominent and well versed in the law of the health care field. Although the AHA provided the author with considerable assistance and support, including staff research by Yvonne N. Bryant, former staff attorney in the Office of the General Counsel, the views are his own and do not necessarily reflect policies or positions of the American Hospital Association.

Richard L. Epstein
Vice-President
American Hospital Association

chapter 1

introduction

Why a special publication on the subject of "informed consent"? This question can best be answered by responding that the issue is highly complex, involving issues of law, morality, and ethics and, further, that it is the cause of continuing controversy among the multiple parties of the health care team in their relation to one another. To oversimplify the concept, it can be said that informed consent is nothing more or less than good medicine. It may involve such highly publicized issues as the army private who is unknowingly administered LSD as part of a CIA experiment or the welfare mother being sterilized without her knowledge or consent. On the day-to-day level of activities, it may mean disclosing to a female patient the possible future risks of pregnancies where a tubal ligation has been performed.

One writer, in the October 1977 issue of *Trustee*, described the concept of informed consent as being the "patient's most important right."

The American Hospital Association, seeking to clarify the relationship between hospital, physician, and patient, published *A Patient's Bill of Rights* in 1972. The document, submitted to hospitals for their consideration, included the following declaration:

> The patient has the right to receive from his physician information necessary to give informed consent prior to the start of any procedure and/or treatment. Except in emergencies, such infor-

1

mation for informed consent, should include but not necessarily be limited to the specific procedure and/or treatment, the medically significant risks involved, and the probable duration of incapacitation. Where medically significant alternatives for care and treatment exist, or when the patient requests information concerning medical alternatives, the patient has the right to such information. The patient also has the right to know the name of the person responsible for the procedures and/or treatment.

This statement summarizes the information that, in the opinion of many courts, a physician must communicate to his patient in order for the patient's consent to treatment to be truly "informed." A simpler definition of informed consent was offered by Justice Blackmun in the case of *Planned Parenthood of Central Missouri v. Danforth.* The plaintiffs in that case objected to a statute that required women, prior to submitting to abortion, to certify in writing that their consent to the procedure is "informed" and freely given. Justice Blackmun stated, in a footnote:

One might well wonder, offhand, just what informed consent of a patient is. The three Missouri federal judges who comprised the three-judge District Court, however, were not concerned, and we are content to accept, as the meaning, the giving of information to the patient as to just what would be done and as to its consequences. To ascribe more meaning than this might well confine the attending physician in an undesired and uncomfortable straitjacket in the practice of his profession. *Planned Parenthood of Central Missouri v. Danforth,* 428 U.S. 52, 67 (1976).

From the viewpoint of the physician, the rhetoric and litigation over the issue of informed consent has constituted not only potential threat of a malpractice claim but also a basic change in the role of the physician. The physician is disturbed by the uncertainty of the definition of physician responsibility and the inability to predict whether the courts will ultimately find that he has fulfilled his duty. The physician's problem is compounded by his inability to determine in advance whether he has properly documented his professional responsibility. Many physicians find intellectual difficulty with the concept that not only does the patient have the right to participate in and control the ultimate medical decision but the patient has the right to make the "wrong medical" decision. Although hospitals have less direct involvement than physicians, their vital concern with informed consent is very evident in the health care field. These concerns are discussed on pages 14-17.

The purpose of this publication, of necessity, is something less than an encyclopedic discourse on all of the nuances of the subject. It is hoped that it will give members of the health care team a basic definition and understanding of the importance of the doctrine as well as appropriate application in the everyday practice of health care. In addition, it provides an up-to-date analysis of both the court cases and statutes on the subject for the reader interested in the technical phases of the law. Also, there is a suggested model statute in chapter 5 and a review of one state's specific experiences in chapter 6.

One last warning to the reader. Despite its earlier origins, the concept of informed consent is an essentially new one in the law (the first case in recent times being in Kansas in 1960) and has not fully matured. What we say today will be modified and changed as the social pattern of action and reaction take place. For example, the statutes seeking to define or limit the application of the doctrine are reactions to the court cases that first declared certain moral and ethical principles relating to medical practice to be a basis for liability in law.

a contemporary
overview

In 1972, the American Hospital Association Board of Trustees approved and released for consideration by its membership a statement entitled *A Patient's Bill of Rights*. This document was widely acclaimed by the media as being a statesmanlike approach to a much misunderstood role. AHA considered the principal purpose of *A Patient's Bill of Rights* as a method of informing the members of the public of their rights within the health care system and of prompting them to seek and utilize these rights. By setting forth these rights in a simple but complete document, the AHA affirmatively called attention of both the public and the health care providers to how far and how rapidly both the interrelationship between the patient and the health care provider had changed.

Included as one of the most important of the identified rights was that of an informed consent. The AHA statement on this issue declared:

> 2. The patient has the right to obtain from his physician complete current information concerning this diagnosis, treatment, and prognosis in terms the patient can be reasonably expected to understand. When it is not medically advisable to give such information to the patient, the information should be made available to an appropriate person in his behalf. He has the right to know by name the physician responsible for coordinating his care.

3. The patient has the right to receive from his physician information necessary to give informed consent prior to the start of any procedure and/or treatment. Except in emergencies, such information for informed consent should include but not necessarily be limited to the specific procedure and/or treatment, the medically significant risks involved, and the probable duration of incapacitation. Where medically significant alternatives for care or treatment exist, or when the patient requests information concerning medical alternatives, the patient has the right to such information. The patient also has the right to know the name of the person responsible for the procedures and/or treatment.

4. The patient has the right to refuse treatment to the extent permitted by law, and to be informed of the medical consequences of his action.

The issue of informed consent is most often raised in medical malpractice cases. If the patient has received a bad result and the issue of negligence is weak, the plaintiff's attorney will allege and seek to prove a lack of informed consent. Such an allegation will not only buttress a weak case on medical negligence but will also help ensure the plaintiff against a sustained demurrer or nonsuit. The most recent report by the All Industry Committee Special Malpractice Review: 1974 Closed Claim Study indicated that a lack of informed consent was alleged in 14 percent of malpractice cases brought. However, it is believed that the practice of pleading the lack of informed consent has materially increased since the 1974 study.

The concern for the lack of informed consent reflects a fundamental change in the relationship between the health care provider and the patient. Superficially, this change in relationship could be described as the age of consumerism in the health field, but to consider this as consumerism is to oversimplify both the complexities and the significance in the change that has occurred. Furthermore, one can observe that the change in relationship has not completed its cycle and that we are only in midstream. During the past 20 years of development of the concept, the emphasis has been the duty of the physician to his patient, on the one hand, and the newly defined (although long recognized) rights of the patient, on the other. It is anticipated that in the future the circle will be completed and emphasis will be on the obligation of the patient to the health care system. The earliest statements on *A Patient's Bill of Rights*[1] included a parallel statement of the patient's responsibility. With the present emphasis on the recognition and codification of the patient's rights in his relationship to the health care system, his reciprocal responsibility for his own health care and his obligation to the health care system have been temporarily overlooked.[2] However, in the recent American Bar Association Commission on Medical Professional Liability report, these reciprocal duties are spelled out.[3] Since these duties have a potentially great impact on the increasing cost of health care, one can expect increasing emphasis on them.

How, then, does the newly expounded concept of informed consent that has developed in the past 20 years in the health field differ from the historic legal doctrine of consent? Historically, a medical consent was merely a granting of permission by a patient or the patient's legal representative to an assault or battery upon the patient. Even though it could be assumed that the fact that the patient was presented to the health care provider for care was, in itself, a consent with the potential of a simple touching or something more significant anticipated, this was not necessarily conclusive proof. The matter of proof of the consent was a potential question that could best be documented by a simple signed consent. As a result, the signing of a broad consent form with no explanation became routine practice in hospitals and doctors' offices. On occasion, the patient or the patient's representative may have signed the form along with a number of other forms routinely without question. The patient did not presume to question the forms. Sometimes the hospital admission clerk or the secretary in the doctor's office would have been medically unqualified to answer any pertinent question. From a legal point of view, the litigated questions related almost entirely to the competency of the signing individual, and these are primarily questions of contract law in the most basic sense.

The practice of medicine has become more complex with far more alternatives to the method of treatment. Furthermore, the potential dangers of various forms of available treatment have become far greater. These factors, coupled with the increased

---

1. Report of the Secretary's Commission on Medical Malpractice, DHEW Publication No. (OS) 73-88, pp. 71-73.
2. AHA. *A Patient's Bill of Rights.* AHA: Chicago, 1972.
3. American Bar Association, 1977 Report of the Commission on Medical Professional Liability, p. 24.

expectations of patients for receiving a miracle cure, have created a new tension between the patient and the health care provider. A further complicating factor is that the patient is no longer dealing with his family physician with whom he has had a long relationship of mutual confidence and trust. In the hospital in particular, the patient faces a bewildering spectrum of specialists and consultants who are often, at best, a vague name and an overwhelming presence.

As a consumer of health services, the patient has the same rights as the consumer of other products to a full and fair disclosure of the product's inherent hazards. The anachronistic legal doctrine of "buyer beware" no longer applies. In addition, there has been increased emphasis on the fiduciary role of such professionals as lawyers, accountants, ministers, and the like, with the physician-patient relationship being described in similar terms. Both federal and state legislatures have also mandated additional burdens of disclosure upon the health care provider, for example, the federal swine flu legislation and various state statutes relating to sterilization and abortion. The requirements for disclosure of the hazards of smoking tobacco are all a part of this social trend. Much greater emphasis is being placed on the disclosure of hazards as distinguished from the actual prohibition of the product or procedure—the most dramatic recent example being the legalization of Laetrile by many state legislatures. In other words, not only does the patient-consumer have the right to know, but legislation may give him the right to exercise his own judgment and to defy all of the scientific and professional judgments to the contrary.

The Patient

All of the above factors and many more have led to the recognition that the patient has the right to participate in decisions affecting his physical and mental welfare, and if the patient is to exercise this right, then the patient must be informed. For this right to be effective, there must also be a correlative duty on the part of the provider to do the informing, and this results in the burden placed upon the health care providers.

Although the following list is not necessarily of a legal nature, the author would define the rights of the patient in this way:

1. The patient should know the nature of his problem and the progress of the diagnosis by the physician. Obviously, this is not

simple in actual practice, as the physician may be exploring a number of alternatives, some of which, though remote, would be extremely alarming to the patient. However, if the patient is to be fully cooperative, the patient must be informed as to major developments in the diagnosis.

2. The patient must be informed as to the alternative courses of treatment as the diagnosing proceeds. Such information must include both the risks and advantages of the alternatives. As a course of treatment is developed, decisions must be made as to when to abandon one course or to adopt another, so that there can be more than one critical decision during a span of time. Obviously, the physician will be expected to recommend a course so that an exposition of the positives as well as the negatives are of equal importance if the confidence of the patient is to be maintained.

3. A patient may properly waive his right to disclosure, but the physician should not overreach in his desire to achieve such a waiver. Many patients believe that they have made their choice by choosing the physician, and they place absolute faith in him to make the difficult decisions. A patient who is mentally coerced into a particular course of treatment will be the one most likely to react to an adverse result and challenge the validity of the consent.

4. The patient should be informed of the degree of risk, including consideration of both probability and severity. If there is a medically significant risk of death or serious injury, this must be exposed to the patient. Of concern to the physician is the fact that such exposition may lead the patient to reject a course of treatment that the physician sincerely believes to be in the best interest of the patient. However, we must keep in mind that the patient in some states may have the legal right to reject a course of treatment even though his physician is absolutely convinced that it is in the best interest of the patient.[4] The physician does have the right to withhold disclosure if, in his judgment, the patient is unable to handle the disclosure and if the disclosure would so affect the patient as to seriously affect his potential recovery. The physician must use reasonable judgment in making this decision.

---

4. See discussion of patient's right to refuse treatment on p. 16.

5. State courts *should* recognize the right of the patient to reject treatment that will sustain life. Whether it is described as the "right to die with dignity" or the right to refuse heroic measures, the ultimate legal and social issue is the right, based upon adequate information, to determine what course of treatment is acceptable. In such a situation it is apparent that the patient must be adequately informed of the consequences of either accepting or rejecting the proposed course of treatment.

Although the above may be considered the big issues from the viewpoint of the patient, there are other issues between the patient and the health care system as a result of the need to inform the patient of matters relating to his case:

1. The patient may not be subjected to investigative or experimental procedures without the patient's consent—and such consent must be an informed one with all of the elements previously described.[5] No health care provider should engage in such procedures without having an established protocol that will ensure appropriate protective measures for the patient. These principles apply to the use of experimental drugs[6] and also to new or innovative procedures in surgery.

2. Participation by a patient in a teaching program is another area of potential conflict if the patient is not properly informed of the advantages and disadvantages of participating in such a program. No longer can we assume that the welfare patient has necessarily given up his right of privacy or waived his right to be treated with consideration simply because he is medically indigent. As more and more paying patients are, of necessity, utilized for teaching purposes, the need for formalized information procedures becomes increasingly important.

3. The patient has the right to be informed as to not only the identity of the practitioner who is responsible for his care but also the identity of those who may perform certain critical procedures.[7] He should not be subjected to surgery by nameless, unaccountable physicians. Although "ghost surgery" has long been declared to be strictly unethical by the American College of Surgeons and the American Medical Association, it has taken

---

5. See item 9 in AHA's *A Patient's Bill of Rights*.
6. FDA Regulations, 21 CFR, Part 310; HEW Regulations, 45 CFR, Part 46.
7. *A Patient's Bill of Rights*.

heroic efforts by the profession to eliminate this commercial practice. However, in the modern context of the teaching hospital, the role of the resident physician, who may assume full responsibility for the surgery of the patient, remains as a knotty problem of communication and disclosure. Fortunately, by the use of highly visible name tags, hospitals are making a major effort to identify personnel not only as to name but also as to professional qualification. The ubiquitous white jacket can be terribly confusing to an already intimidated patient. If the procedure involves a team approach, the patient should know the matter of the interrelation between the ancillary specialties, such as anesthesiology, radiology, pathology, and so forth.

4. Last, and perhaps one of the most controversial issues in relation to the patient's right to be informed, is the possible right of the patient to unlimited access to his medical record. The law on this issue is split. Some states recognize an almost unlimited right; others set up some barriers. Here is a classical conflict of the right of the patient to know and be informed and the need to maintain a continuous record of the diagnosis and treatment of the patient without fear of its being improperly used. For a record to be most useful from a professional point of view, it should include all objective observations including the pattern of diagnosis, which may require reference to and ultimate elimination of potentials, which, if known to the patient, would be highly disturbing. To permit the patient unlimited access to such material without some guidance can have a chilling effect on those required to maintain the record. The record of a mental health diagnosis can be particularly sensitive. Ultimately, the courts or the legislature will settle this conflict of social needs.[8]

The Physician

The right of the patient must be reflected in a duty by the physician. The term *physician* is emphasized rather than *health care provider* because in nearly all situations it is the physician who is primarily responsible for the informed consent. The attending physician is primarily responsible for the patient's care and as such is in the ultimate fiduciary capacity to the patient. All other participants of the health care team must be supportive of the attending physician's efforts.

---

8. *Gotkin v. Miller,* 514 F. 2d 125 (2d Cir. 1975).

The law is clear in that the patient's physician has the primary duty to communicate with the patient. The law does not say how he must communicate. In other words, he has considerable leeway in the methodology he may use. The method used will vary with the specialty as well as the approach the individual physician can use most effectively. The critical point is that the method used must be comprehensible to the patient. Communication involves a giving out of information in a manner comprehensible to the other party. This means overcoming language barriers both as to foreign tongue and as to excessive use of technical terminology, which may be equally incomprehensible.

The individual physician may use visual aids, tape recordings, written pamphlets, personal explanation, or any other device or devices that will be comprehensible to the patient. Three critical elements must be considered:

1. The method of communication must be comprehensible, as far as can be determined, to the particular patient involved.

2. The patient must be given an adequate opportunity to ask questions or to indicate the need for further explanation.

3. The patient has the right to terminate or waive the explanation, but should not be encouraged to do so by the physician.

Having communicated with the patient, the physician then needs to establish a record that the communication has taken place. This is not a substitute for the communication itself but is a legal record to support the facts at a distant later date. Although many legal advisers prefer an effective oral dialog, a summary of which is immediately entered into the physician's office record or on the hospital chart, this method is not exclusive. What is not recommended is for a physician to rely on the fact that he always discusses such matters with his patients even though he never records it. Unfortunately, it must be assumed that even when acting in the best of faith, the patient's or even the physician's recall of the discussion may well be totally lost or, at best, inaccurate. For this reason, the physician must rely on his own record to establish the basic facts, or to refresh his memory.

Obviously, the nature of the procedure, whether it is emergency or elective, and the previous relationship with the physician all have a bearing on the protocol to be followed. What must be emphasized is that although the physician can delegate certain elemᴖnts of the patient education process, it is his ultimate responsibility to ensure that the patient has given an informed consent.

In absence of statute or reimbursement regulation, there is no requirement that surgical consents be in writing or signed. They can be oral or even implied. A signed written consent merely provides meaningful and credible evidence that consent was in fact obtained. Except in emergency situations, hospital attorneys do advise their clients to routinely get written consents. Also, there is no magic in the form being labeled "informed consent" or containing elaborate recitals of disclosure, if the information was not in fact supplied.

A special problem to the physician is the legal capacity of the patient to give an informed consent. A minor, in many situations, may not be able to give any consent, let alone an informed consent. The same limitations may apply to senile, mentally ill, or mentally deficient patients or the patient who is under sedation. Special problems exist in the emergency room or when the patient is in shock or severe pain.

The physician must also be aware of any special legal requirements pertaining to consents to specific procedures, such as sterilization or abortion. A relatively new problem is the consideration of a requirement, proposed primarily as a cost containment measure, for a second opinion on surgical or other costly procedures being applied under some health insurance programs.

Within the hospital setting, the attending physician has certain duties that may or may not be referred to other physicians on the health care team. For example, the choice of the anesthetic agent and the appropriate explanation to the patient can be of critical importance. Many major malpractice cases have revolved around this issue. Similarly, the potential dangers of certain diagnostic and therapeutic procedures must be explained and resolved with the patient. Although such explanations can be delegated to another member of the physician team, such as the radiologist, anesthesiologist, and so forth, clear assurance of their assumption of this responsibility must be established. The failure to create clear lines of responsibility within a medical staff can create not only serious friction but, more importantly, the potential of serious injury to the patient. Such potential is inherent in the increasing complexity of medical care and the expansion of specialization.

The extent of communication to the patient lies in the professional judgment area. Some courts have stated that the physician need not engage in a medical school minicourse and need not cover matters of general public knowledge. In some states, the standard must be established by a competent expert witness as to the standards of the applicable medical community, but in others the jury can speculate on the standard of the "reasonable patient." Each physician should acquaint himself with the standards for his particular state.

The Role of the Hospital and Hospital Personnel

Although many physicians would prefer to delegate the responsibility for obtaining the informed consent to hospital personnel, legally and ethically this is not an answer. Historically, many hospitals have obtained the patient's signature to a surgical consent as a protection to both the hospital and the surgeon. Some physicians find it difficult to understand why this relatively simple and efficient process has to be extended to include a formal communication on their part so that they must now be burdened with the additional matter of communication and any red tape of record keeping.

As previously stated, hospital personnel who are not physicians have neither the responsibility nor the special information necessary to establish the two-way communication with the patient that will assure the health care team that the consent of the patient is informed. Such communication would require the hospital personnel not only to be fully familiar with the patient's history but also with the procedure, complications, and reasons why the physician intended to use the particular procedure. Many of these matters are solely within the knowledge of the physician and may be a part of his fiduciary relationship with his patient.

The hospital does have a supportive role. On this subject, the JCAH has recently stated:

> Evidence of appropriate informed consent. The medical record shall contain evidence of the patient's informed consent for any procedure or treatment for which it is appropriate. This information should include the identity of the patient, the date, the procedure or treatment to be rendered (in layman terminology when possible), the name(s) of the individual(s) who will perform the procedure or administer the treatment, authorization for anesthesia if indicated, an indication that alternate means of therapy

and the possibility of risks or complications have been explained to the patient, and authorization for disposition of any tissue or body parts as indicated. The signature of the patient or other individual empowered to give consent should be witnessed. The practitioner with clinical privileges who informs the patient and obtains the consent should be identified in the medical record. A hospital policy and procedure, consistent with legal requirements, shall be developed to apply in certain procedures such as sterilization or abortion, or in situations when appropriate informed consent cannot be given, such as in the case of a patient who is unconscious or an unaccompanied unemancipated minor. The need for documentation of special aspects of consent, such as for patient photographs, or for observation of a surgical procedure or for other educational purposes, shall be determined by the individual facility and shall be consistent with any legal requirements.[9]

Properly interpreted, this should place the burden upon the accredited hospital to establish a clear protocol within its medical staff as to the respective responsibilities for obtaining informed consents. For example, the relationships between the surgeons and anesthesiologists should be spelled out as well as the responsibility between the obstetrician and the pediatrician as to the newborn and other similar shared responsibilities.

The hospital should consider placing in its consent forms or in the explanatory literature given to patients an explanation of the patient's right to know and right to participate in decisions affecting his care. A locally adapted version of *A Patient's Bill of Rights* published by the AHA (or the similar statement required by law in a few states) will partially fulfill this role. Above all, the hospital should continuously train all hospital personnel who have patient contact to be alert to any indication that a particular patient is confused or uninformed as to what is to happen to him. Such fact should be immediately reported to the appropriate physician for action and the fact of the report charted.

In like manner, the hospital medical staff can provide a useful service in educating its own members as to their professional and legal requirements of informed consent. Also, an occasional presentation to the medical staff by the hospital attorney can be very useful.

---

9. *JCAH Accreditation Manual for Hospitals,* February 1978 edition, p. 65.

The hospital can perform an important role in patient education through the use of seminars, visual aids, and the like, to provide detailed explanations as to certain diseases or procedures as a backup to the physician's own explanation. Much useful material can be made available on a group basis that cannot be provided by the individual physician. Similarly, follow-up educational activity, either predischarge or postdischarge, will assist the patient in understanding the nature of his problems and treatment and, above all, the importance in following the regimen recommended by his physician.

In special circumstances, there may be requirements placed on the health care institution for obtaining the execution of special forms. This can relate to government-financed programs or such socially controversial issues as sterilization and abortion. The hospital must also establish any necessary protocol in connection with research or experimental drugs or modalities.

The hospital should clearly identify its personnel as to both name and profession so that the patient will be informed as to who is treating him and the person's qualifications.

Where feasible, the hospital should also undertake to maintain communication with responsible relatives, particularly during such periods as the patient may be unable to make rational decisions on his own behalf. The hospital may be the only way that such individual or the patient himself can reach, much less communicate with, his physician.

Ultimately, if there is a complete breakdown in the communication between the patient and his physician, the hospital may have to request the chief of staff or department head to intervene. Similarly, the hospital has a legal duty to ensure compliance with court orders as to treatment. Conceivably, there may even be a duty to initiate an appropriate request for a court order when, on the basis of sound medical judgment and applicable state law, it is believed to be in the patient's best interests. Unfortunately, laws of the states vary as to which persons and under what circumstances treatment may be refused. (See AHA's suggested statement on the *Right of the Patient To Refuse Treatment*.) The hospital attorney should be consulted as to state law applicable to particular facts.

Where the hospital attorney is of the firm opinion that state law permits a "no-code" order, the hospital, through its medical staff, must establish the protocol for utilization of "no code" orders. Such protocol must specify the medical circumstances under which such orders may be entered, the nature of patient or family involvement, and so forth. These are all elements of the informed consent process.

It is not the purpose of this book to cover all of the issues of the law of consents. These legal problems continue together with the new ones that are developing as the result of the utilization of physician's assistants or nurse practitioners, for example. The question of the duration of a particular consent or the method of revocation of a consent must still be faced.

It is hoped that the adjustments being made in the relationship between health care provider and patient through better information and mutual understanding will constitute a very positive force in not only improving the quality of medical care, but also in minimizing the frictions that so disastrously affect the role of the health care provider and the public.

This chapter has carefully avoided the use of court citations or the analysis of the developing legal doctrines as set forth by recent case decisions or by statutes. However, this chapter should form a basis for understanding the problems with which the courts and legislatures have had to struggle in an attempt to develop a rational framework of legal doctrine when doing it on a case-by-case approach. Although the courts have seemed to adopt some quite arbitrary and irrational positions on some medicolegal issues, the overall pattern of decisions in the informed consent area have been by and large constructive and rational. When the courts have gone too far, then remedial legislative action may be indicated as covered by chapters 4 and 5.

chapter 3

informed consent in the courts

The Development of the Doctrine

The modern doctrine of informed consent is a logical out-growth of the common law rule that an unauthorized operation will subject the physician[1] to liability in tort to the patient.[2] Although modern decisions have utilized the negligence framework for determining such liability, the doctrine developed under the legal rubric of "assault and battery."[3]

---

1. It should be emphasized at the outset that the informed consent doctrine imposes its primary obligations upon the physician rather than the hospital. We have not found any case in which a hospital was found liable for failing to obtain an informed consent to treatment. However, there is dicta to the effect that such liability might arise if the hospital knew or should have known that a private physician was undertaking to treat a patient in the hospital without obtaining informed consent. *Fiorentino v. Wenger,* 19 N.Y. 2d 407, 418, 227 N.E. 2d 296, 301, 280 N.Y.S.2d 373, 381 (1967).

2. While the patient will normally be the plaintiff in an informed consent action, a recent New York decision indicates that a child may also be entitled to bring such a suit for injuries sustained during his delivery. *Shack v. Holland,* 789 Misc. 2d 78, 389 N.Y.S. 2d 988 (1976). The trial court in *Shack* declared that an "unborn plaintiff" is within the class of persons protected by the informed consent doctrine, and is therefore entitled to derivative protection under the doctrine.

3. See Prosser, *Torts,* §18 (4th ed. 1971). The recent use of negligence theory is not, as some have suggested, a substitute for battery theory, but rather represents the development of a new cause of action based on the recognition that physicians have an affirmative duty of disclo-

19

Four cases are often cited as progenitors of the informed consent doctrine. The first is *Mohr v. Williams*,[4] wherein the defendant physician performed an operation upon the plaintiff's left ear despite having obtained consent only to perform a similar operation for her right ear. The court held that unless a jury found that the patient had consented, either expressly or impliedly, to the challenged operation, "the act of defendant amounted at least to a technical assault and battery."[5] Similarly, in *Pratt v. Davis*,[6] the court affirmed a judgment for "trespass to the person" (*i.e.*, battery) as the result of the removal of the plaintiff's ovaries and uterus without her consent. In *Rolater v. Strain*,[7] it was held that the removal of a bone from the plaintiff's foot without her consent —indeed, contrary to her express prior disapproval—constituted an actionable battery. Finally, in *Schloendorff v. Society of New York Hospitals*,[8] a fibroid tumor was removed from the plaintiff's abdomen without her consent during a purportedly "diagnostic" procedure. In the course of his decision in Schloendorff, Judge Cardozo made an observation that is obligatorily quoted in almost every treatise on informed consent:

> Every human being of adult years and sound mind has a right to determine what shall be done with his own body; and a surgeon who performs an operation without his patient's consent commits an assault, for which he is liable in damages. . . . This is true, except in cases of emergency where the patient is unconscious, and where it is necessary to operate before consent can be obtained.[9]

As a review of the preceding cases shows, all are united by the common factual circumstances of an operation performed without prior disclosure as to its nature or scope. This is different, both in kind and degree, from the situation where the nature and scope of the operation are explained to the patient, but where possible

---

sure. In at least one jurisdiction, the duty of disclosure is not recognized, and no cause of action exists for the failure to disclose the risks of, and alternatives to, a proposed medical procedure. *See Young v. Yarn,* 136 Ga. App. 737, 222 S.E.2d 113 (1975).

4. 95 Minn. 261, 104 N.W. 12 (1905).
5. *Id.* at 271, 104 N.W. at 16 (1905).
6. 224 Ill. 300, 79 N.E. 562 (1906).
7. 39 Okla. 572, 137 P. 96 (1913).
8. 211 N.Y. 125, 105 N.E. 92 (1914), *overruled on other grounds, Bing v. Thunig,* 2 N.Y. 2d 656, 143 N.E. 2d 3, 163 N.Y.S. 2d 3 (1957).
9. *Id.* at 126, 105 N.E. at 93 (1914).

complications and alternatives are not disclosed.[10] It is this distinction that furnishes a principled means of separating the causes of action for battery and for negligence.[11]

Despite scattered statements in the early consent cases regarding a duty to disclose the risks of a medical procedure,[12] it was not until the decision in *Natanson v. Kline*[13] that the issue was discussed at length. *Natanson* involved a malpractice action brought

---

10. This distinction is emphasized in Plante, *An Analysis of "Informed Consent,"* 36 Fordham L. Rev. 639, 650 (1968). Professor Plante states that a line should be drawn between cases involving a touching of a substantially different character as represented and cases involving a touching exactly as represented but where collateral risks were not disclosed. While the failure to disclose risks may be deemed to vitiate any consent given to the operation, it is more convenient to view the latter cases as the true "informed consent" decisions, rather than as an inseparable part of the broader consent requirement doctrine.

11. *See Cobbs v. Grant,* 8 Cal. 3d 229, 240, 502 P.2d 1, 8, 104 Cal. Rptr. 505, 512 (1972):

> The battery theory should be reserved for those circumstances when a doctor performs an operation to which the patient has not consented. When the patient gives permission to perform one type of treatment and the doctor performs another, the requisite element of deliberate intent to deviate from the consent given is present. However, when the patient consents to certain treatment and the doctor performs that treatment but an undisclosed inherent complication with a low probability occurs, no intentional deviation from the consent given appears; rather, the doctor in obtaining consent may have failed to meet his due care duty to disclose pertinent information. In that situation the action should be pleaded in negligence.

Also, see Plante, *supra* note 10.

12. *See, e.g., Hunt v. Bradshaw,* 242 N.C. 517, 523, 88 S.E.2d 762, 766 (1955):

> Failure to explain the risk involved, therefore, may be considered a mistake on the part of the surgeon, but under the facts cannot be deemed such want of ordinary care as to import liability.

Also, *see Salgo v. Leland Stanford Jr. Univ. Bd. of Trustees,* 154 Cal. App. 2d 560, 578, 317 P.2d 170, 181 (1957), wherein the court made the following observation:

> A physician violates his duty to his patient and subjects himself to liability if he withholds any facts which are necessary to form the basis of an intelligent consent by the patient to the proposed treatment. Likewise the physician may not minimize the known dangers of a procedure or operation in order to induce his patient's consent.

Some commentators consider *Salgo* to be the genesis of the modern doctrine of informed consent. *See* Comment, *New Trends in Informed Consent?,* 54 Neb. L. Rev. 66, 68 (1975); Plante, *supra* note 10.

13. 186 Kan. 393, 350 P.2d 1093 (1960).

against a hospital and a physician for injuries sustained as the result of cobalt radiation therapy. Although the complaint did allege negligence in performing the therapy, a further count asserted that the defendant physician "failed to warn the appellant the course of treatment which he undertook to administer involved great risk of bodily injury or death."[14] Citing the case of *Salgo v. Leland Stanford Jr. University Bd. of Trustees*,[15] the court held that the physician "was obligated to make a reasonable disclosure to the appellant of the nature and probable consequences of the suggested or recommended cobalt irradiation treatment, and he was also obligated to make a reasonable disclosure of the dangers within his knowledge which were incident to, or possible in, the treatment he proposed to administer."[16] However, the court further noted that his duty of disclosure is limited to those disclosures that a reasonable medical practitioner would make under the same or similar circumstances.

Just two days after the *Natanson* case was decided, the Supreme Court of Missouri dealt with the same informed consent issue in *Mitchell v. Robinson*.[17] There, the plaintiff brought an action for negligence arising from the administration of insulin shock treatments. The plaintiff alleged that a risk inherent in such treatments are convulsions resulting in bone fractures, but that he was not informed of this risk prior to his therapy. Relying in part on a few preceding cases and in part on a "thoughtful" law review article,[18] the court declared:

> In the particular circumstances of this record, considering the nature of Mitchell's illness and this rather new and radical procedure with its rather high incidence of serious and permanent injuries not connected with the illness, the doctors owed their patient in possession of his faculties the duty to inform him gen-

14. *Id.* at 400, 350 P.2d at 1099 (1960).
15. 154 Cal.App.2d 560, 317 P.2d 170 (1957). See note 12, *supra*.
16. 186 Kan. at 410, 350 P.2d at 1106.
17. 334 S.W.2d 11 (Mo. 1960).
18. The article to which the court referred, entitled "A Reappraisal of Liability for Unauthorized Medical Treatment," was written by Professor Allan H. McCoid in 41 Minn. L. Rev. 381 (1957). One of the recommendations made by Professor McCoid in that article was the grounding of malpractice liability upon a failure by the doctor to make a reasonable disclosure of all significant facts concerning a proposed operation. It is interesting to note that the McCoid article was also cited in *Natanson*, albeit in a more cursory manner.

erally of the possible serious collateral hazards; and in the detailed circumstances there was a submissible fact issue of whether the doctors were negligent in failing to inform him of the dangers of shock therapy.[19]

The combined legal effect of the *Mitchell* and *Natanson* decisions was to establish a clear common law duty to disclose the risks of medical treatment. The combined practical effect was to open the floodgates to a rash of informed consent claims.[20]

Battery versus Negligence

While some courts have permitted a cause of action for lack of informed consent to be brought under a battery theory,[21] modern decisions normally reserve that theory for situations where the defendant physician has failed to disclose the nature or character of the operation to be performed.[22] The cases in which the battery theory is properly applied include: where the physician obtains consent to perform an operation, but either exceeds the scope of that consent,[23] misrepresents the severity of

19. 334 S.W.2d at 19.

20. Since the mid-1950s, the frequency with which informed consent issues have been litigated has increased both absolutely and relative to nearly every other issue litigated in malpractice actions. *See* Schneyer, *Informed Consent and the Danger of Bias in the Formation of Medical Disclosure Practices,* 1976 Wis. L. Rev. 124, 142. Even so, however, the doctrine was only discussed in 6.6 percent of the reported malpractice appeals between 1961 and 1971. *See* Riskin, *Informed Consent: Looking for the Action,* 1975 U. Ill. L. Forum 580, 592; Curran, W. J., "How Lawyers Handle Medical Malpractice Cases: An Analysis of the Important Medicolegal Study," NCHSR Report Series, Department of HEW, Publication No. (HRA) 76-3152, 1976, at page 20-21.

21. *See, e.g., Berkey v. Anderson,* 1 Cal.App.3d 790, 803-804, 82 Cal. Rptr. 67, 76-77 (1970) ; *Cooper v. Roberts,* 220 Pa. Super. Ct. 260, 286 A.2d 647 (1971).

22. *See* Note, *Informed Consent Liability,* 26 Drake L. Rev. 696, 699 (1977) ; Comment, *A Doctor's Duty to Inform—Holland v. Sisters of Saint Joseph of Peace,* 1974 Utah L. Rev. 851. Also, *see Downer v. Veilleux,* 322 A.2d 82, 89 (Me. 1974) :

> But, the "majority trend" is towards treating the physician's failure to disclose as merely another variety of medical negligence, reserving the battery theory for cases in which the treatment is either against the patient's will or substantially at variance with the consent given.

23. *E.g., Bang v. Charles T. Miller Hospital,* 251 Minn. 427, 88 N.W.2d 186 (1958) (physician failed to disclose that prostate operation required severance of the patient's spermatic cords).

the operation,[24] or performs an operation of a substantially different nature.[25] On the other hand, negligence theory is generally attached to claims alleging a failure to disclose potential complications or alternative methods of treatment.[26] Nevertheless, it is certainly conceivable that a given court might allow a risk disclosure action to be brought in battery or might fail to recognize that an unauthorized treatment suit is fundamentally a matter of risk disclosure. For that reason, it is important to recognize some of the more significant implications in phrasing the cause of action in terms of battery vis-à-vis negligence.

One effect of choosing between negligence and battery liability is that the pertinent statute of limitations will thereby be determined. In a number of jurisdictions, the statute of limitations governing malpractice will differ from the statute regulating assault and battery actions.[27] Not only may the statutes prescribe different limitation periods for battery and negligence, but the date that the cause of action accrues may also vary. For example, whereas actions in Kentucky for battery and negligent malpractice both have a one-year limitation period from the time the cause of action accrued, the cause of action for malpractice is not deemed to accrue until the injury is discovered or should have been discovered.[28]

An interesting case in point is *Terry v. Albany Medical Center Hospital.*[29] *Terry* involved an action to recover damages resulting from a coronary arteriography. The complaint contained counts

24. A novel case in point is presented by *Cathemer v. Hunter,* 27 Ariz. App. 780, 558 P.2d 975 (1976). There, the plaintiff brought a battery action alleging lack of consent to the hip prosthesis operation performed by the defendant physician. Despite the fact that he had specifically authorized that operation, the court found for the plaintiff on the ground that he was mistakenly led to believe that a hip prosthesis involved a total hip replacement.

25. *E.g., Schloendorff v. Society of New York Hospitals,* 211 N.Y. 125, 105 N.E. 92 (1914). See the text accompanying note 8, *supra.*

26. *See Cobbs v. Grant, supra* note 11; *Wilkinson v. Vesey,* 110 R.I. 606, 620, 295 A.2d 676, 686 (1972).

27. Louisell and Williams state that 31 states and the District of Columbia have separate assault and battery limitation periods. D. Louisell and H. Williams, *Medical Malpractice,* ¶13.04 (1973).

28. Compare Ky. Rev. Stat. §413.140(1)(a) (Supp. 1976) (battery) with Ky. Rev. Stat. §413.140(1)(e) and Ky. Rev. Stat. §413.140(2) (Supp. 1976) (negligent malpractice).

29. 78 Misc. 2d 1035, 359 N.Y.S. 2d 235 (1974).

phrased both in negligence and assault alleging lack of informed consent. The court held the assault count barred by a one-year statute of limitations, but allowed the negligence claim to stand because the applicable limitation period was three years.

Another upshot of the legal theory employed in an informed consent suit is the amount of damages available to the plaintiff. In a negligence action, compensable damages are limited to those resulting from a materialization of the undisclosed risks.[30] This is a much more limited damage measure than that theoretically available in battery,[31] where the plaintiff is entitled to recover for the wrongful touching,[32] for all injuries resulting from the touching, and perhaps even for punitive damages.[33]

Similarly, the burden of proving causation is more onerous under a negligence theory. The reason is that the plaintiff is required to show that but for the nondisclosure, he would not have consented to the operation.[34] Needless to say, this requirement becomes very difficult to satisfy when the physician can prove that the treatment or operation performed was "medically necessary."[35]

In battery, however, there is no "but for" test. Instead, the plaintiff need only show that the operation was performed without his consent.[36] This criterion is satisfied where the patient had

---

30. *See* note 79, *infra.*

31. Even so, it has been argued that the measure of damages for negligence is too broad and should be restricted to the monetary value of the difference between the patient's condition with no treatment and his condition after the undisclosed risk materialized.

32. An established principle of tort law is that the victim of a battery is entitled at least to nominal damages if the wrongful touching did not have any harmful consequences. Prosser, *Torts,* §9 (4th ed. 1971). Some commentators have criticized the use of negligence theory for its failure to award such nominal damages as "compensation for violation of the patient's dignitary interest." Riskin, *supra* note 20 at 589.

33. Riskin, *supra* note 20 at 584.

34. *See, e.g., Fogal v. Genesee Hospital,* 41 A.D.2d 468, 473-474, 344 N.Y.S.2d 552, 559-560 (1973). Also, see the discussion of causation at the text accompanying notes 79-84, *infra.*

35. Indeed, if a reasonable man standard is used to predict the patient's behavior if full disclosure had been made, it is hard to imagine liability being assessed for any treatment that appeared to be needed. See the text accompanying notes 81-85, *infra.*

36. *See, e.g., Rolater v. Strain,* 39 Okla. 1572, 137 P. 96 (1913).

consented to medical treatment, but that consent was vitiated by inadequate disclosure.[37]

Finally, the method of proof required for negligence may create a greater obstacle for the plaintiff than he would face in a battery action. This derives from the obligation in many jurisdictions that the plaintiff furnish expert medical testimony to show that the defendant physician breached his duty of full disclosure.[38] There is no corresponding requirement in battery,[39] perhaps due in part to the relative paucity of battery cases that have been based on risk disclosure.

From the preceding discussion, it can be seen that the negligence framework is the more restrictive from the standpoint of the plaintiff and is in accordance with the recent trend of the cases.[40]

Aspects of the Negligence Theory

Scope of the Disclosure Duty

The Professional Standard

The early negligence cases almost invariably linked the scope of the physician's disclosure duty with standards adopted

---

37. *See, e.g., Fogal v. Genesee Hospital,* 41 A.D.2d 468, 473, 344 N.Y.S.2d 552, 559 (1973); *Bowers v. Talmage,* 159 So.2d 888, 889 (Fla. Dist. Ct. App. 1963):

    Unless a person who gives consent to an operation knows its dangers and the degree of danger, a "consent" does not represent a choice and is ineffectual.

38. This requirement is described at the text accompanying notes 46 and 47, *infra.*

39. *See Riskin, supra* note 20 at 585; *Cobbs v. Grant,* 8 Cal.3d 229, 240, 502 P.2d 1, 8, 104 Cal. Rptr. 505, 512 (1972):

    [E]xpert opinion as to community standard is not required in a battery count, in which the patient must merely prove failure to give informed consent and a mere touching absent consent.

40. *See, e.g., Cobbs v. Grant, supra* note 11; *Wilkinson v. Vesey,* 110 R.I. 606, 621, 295 A.2d 676, 686 (1972); *Nishi v. Hartwell,* 52 Haw. 188, 191, 473 P.2d 116, 118-119, *reh. den.,* 52 Haw. 296 (1970); *Downer v. Veilleux,* 322 A.2d 82, 89 (Me. 1974).

    Several reasons have been advanced for this phenomenon. These include: (1) battery is commonly perceived as involving an act of an antisocial nature; (2) the act complained of in informed consent cases is not within the traditional idea of "contact" or "touching"; (3) the failure to inform is generally not an intentional act and is thus inconsistent with the intentionality requirement for battery; (4) the physician's malpractice insurance may not cover assault and battery; and (5) informed consent actions do not appear to be appropriate cases for punitive damages awards. *Trogun v. Fruchtman,* 58 Wis.2d 569, 599-600, 207 N.W.2d 297, 313 (1973).

by the medical profession. Thus, in *Natanson v. Kline*,[41] the court stated:

> The duty of the physician to disclose, however, is limited to those disclosures which a reasonable medical practitioner would make under the same or similar circumstances.[42]

Most of the courts that apply the "professional standard" refer to the practice of doctors in the same or a similar community or locality.[43] Others, such as *Natanson*, require disclosures that correspond to those made by a "reasonable medical practitioner."[44] Still others refer simply to disclosures that conform with "prevailing medical practice."[45] Use of the "professional" standard imposes on plaintiffs the burden of proving the nature and scope of customary practice. This normally requires that the plaintiff present expert medical testimony to show the existence of a disclosure duty.[46] Absent such testimony, a dismissal or directed verdict may be entered against the plaintiff.[47]

---

41. 186 Kan. 393, 350 P.2d 1093 (1960).

42. *Id.* at 409, 350 P.2d at 1106 (1960).

43. *Pegram v. Sisco*, 460 F.Supp. 776 (W.D. Ark. 1976); *Stauffer v. Karabin*, 30 Colo.App. 357, 364, 492 P.2d 862, 865 (1971); *DiFilippo v. Preston*, 53 Del. 539, 549-550, 173 A.2d 333, 339 (1961); *Ditlow v. Kaplan*, 181 So.2d 226, 228 (Fla. Dist. Ct. App. 1966); *Haggerty v. McCarthy*, 344 Mass. 136, 141, 181 N.E.2d 562, 566 (1962); *Roberts v. Young*, 369 Mich. 133, 138-140, 119 N.W.2d 627, 629-30 (1963); *Ross v. Hodges*, 234 So.2d 905, 909 (Miss. 1970); *Negaard v. Estate of Feda*, 152 Mont. 47, 56, 446 P.2d 436, 441 (1968); *Kaplan v. Haines*, 96 N.J. Super. 242, 257, 232 A.2d 840, 848 (1967); *Butler v. Berkeley*, 25 N.C.App. 325, 342, 213 S.E.2d 571, 582 (1975); *Wilson v. Scott*, 412 S.W.2d 299, 302 (Tex. 1967); *Ficklin v. Macfarlane*, 550 P.2d 1295 (Utah 1976); *Govin v. Hunter*, 374 P.2d 421, 424 (Wyo. 1962).

44. *Ohligschlager v. Proctor Community Hospital*, 6 Ill.App.3d 81, 88, 283 N.E.2d 86, 89-90 (1972); *Grosjean v. Spencer*, 258 Iowa 685, 691-692, 140 N.W.2d 139, 143 (1966); *Aiken v. Clary*, 396 S.W.2d 668, 674 (Mo. 1965); *ZeBarth v. Swedish Hospital Medical Center*, 81 Wash. 2d 12, 24, 499 P.2d 1, 9 (1972).

45. *Reidesser v. Nelson*, 11 Ariz. 542, 545, 534 P.2d 1052, 1054 (1975); *Bly v. Rhoads*, 216 Va. 645, 651, 222 S.E.2d 783, 788 (1976).

46. *E.g., Grosjean v. Spencer*, 258 Iowa 685, 140 N.W.2d 139 (1966); *Hart v. Van Zandt*, 399 S.W.2d 791 (Tex. 1965). Also, *see* Annot., 52 A.L.R.3d 1084 (1973).

47. *See, e.g., Govin v. Hunter*, 374 P.2d 421, 424 (Wyo. 1962); *Green v. Hussey*, 127 Ill.App.2d 174, 262 N.E.2d 156 (1970).

    However, some courts have permitted the plaintiff to establish the disclosure duty by examining the defendant physician. *See, e.g., Wilson v. Scott*, 412 S.W.2d 299 (Tex. 1967).

The expert testimony requirement has been subjected to considerable criticism by legal commentators.[48] First, it has been suggested that allowing the medical profession to set its own standard creates the danger of insufficient self-regulation.[49] Second, there may not be a "community medical standard" because of disagreement among physicians as to the risks to be disclosed and the alternative treatments to be described.[50] Third, even if a community standard does exist, it may be difficult to establish due to the reluctance of some physicians to testify against their colleagues.[51] Finally, it has been argued that the manner in which medical services are financed, together with the social goals of good health and medical innovation, tends to produce a bias in favor of underdisclosure among doctors in general, thereby making a community medical standard for disclosure inadequate.[52]

The Material Risk Standard

While the professional standard remains the majority rule in the United States,[53] the modern trend is toward an approach that

---

48. *See* Comment, *Informed Consent: A New Standard for Texas*, 8 St. Mary's L. J. 499 (1976).

49. *See Cooper v. Roberts*, 220 Pa. Super Ct. 260, 267, 286 A.2d 647, 650 (1971):

> As the patient must bear the expense, pain and suffering of any injury from medical treatment, his right to know all material facts pertaining to the proposed treatment cannot be dependent upon the self-imposed standards of the medical profession.

In *Wilkinson v. Vesey*, 110 R.I. 606, 624, 295 A.2d 676, 687 (1972), the court points out that whereas in the ordinary malpractice case the physician and patient had a common goal (*viz.*, a cured patient), no such assumption can be made in the informed consent situation. Thus, absent the imposition of tort liability, there is no incentive for the physician to disclose information.

50. *See Wilkinson v. Vesey*, 110 R.I. 606, 623, 295 A.2d 676, 687 (1972); *Canterbury v. Spence*, 464 F.2d 772, 783 (D.C. Cir. 1972).

51. *See, e.g., Huffman v. Lindquist*, 37 Cal.2d 465, 484, 234 P.2d 34, 46 (1951) (Carter, J., dissenting); *Cooper v. Roberts*, 220 Pa. Super. Ct. 260, 267, 286 A.2d 647, 650 (1971):

> Finally, as a practical matter, we must consider the plaintiff's difficulty in finding a physician who would breach the "community of silence" by testifying against the interest of one of his professional colleagues.

52. *See* Schneyer, *Informed Consent and the Danger of Bias in the Formation of Medical Disclosure Practices*, 1976 Wis. L. Rev. 124.

53. *See* Comment, *Informed Consent in Kentucky After the Medical Malpractice Insurance and Claims Act of 1976*, 65 Ky. L. J. 524, 530 (1976).

imposes a more extensive duty upon the physician. That approach measures the duty to disclose in absolute, rather than relative, terms by requiring that all significant or material risks and alternatives be described to the patient. The development of this "material risk" standard is largely attributable to two cases decided in 1972, *Canterbury v. Spence*[54] and *Cobbs v. Grant*.[55]

In *Canterbury*, the defendant physician performed a laminectomy on the plaintiff without disclosing the possibility of resulting paralysis. The day after the operation, the plaintiff fell from his unattended hospital bed. Shortly thereafter, he noticed that the lower half of his body was paralyzed. While his condition eventually improved, the plaintiff never fully regained his normal preoperative condition.

Although the plaintiff's complaint against the defendant physician and hospital alleged several counts of malpractice, the seminal importance of the *Canterbury* decision derives from its extended discussion of the issue of informed consent. The court began that discussion by noting that the use of a disclosure standard created by the medical community is fundamentally inconsistent with the basis of the informed consent doctrine: *viz.*, the patient's right of self-determination on particular therapy.[56] According to the court, the ability to make an intelligent decision requires that all "material"[57] information be disclosed regarding "the inherent and potential hazards of the proposed treatment, the alternatives to that treatment, if any, and the results likely if the patient remains untreated."[58]

---

54. 464 F.2d 772 (D.C. Cir. 1972).

55. *Cobbs v. Grant,* 8 Cal.3d 229, 502 P.2d 1, 104 Cal.Rptr. 505, 1972.

56. *Id.* at 784. However, the court did emphasize that the idea of informed consent should not be carried to the extreme of requiring patient *comprehension* of the risks and alternatives disclosed. For a detailed discussion of the disclosure-understanding dichotomy, see Miesel, *The Expansion of Liability for Medical Accidents: From Negligence to Strict Liability by Way of Informed Consent,* 56 Neb. L. Rev. 51, 113-123 (1977).

57. 464 F.2d at 786. The court settles on disclosure of material risks rather than "full disclosure" because it is "obviously prohibitive and unrealistic to expect physicians to discuss with their patients every risk of proposed treatment—no matter how small or remote—and generally unnecessary from the patient's viewpoint as well." *Id. Accord, Williams v. Menehan,* 191 Kan. 6, 8, 379 P.2d 292, 294 (1963).

58. 464 F.2d at 787. If the proposed operation is novel or unorthodox, that fact should also be revealed to the patient. *See Fiorentino v. Wenger,*

With respect to what constitutes "materiality," the court cited the following definition:

A risk is thus material when a reasonable person, in what the physician knows or should know to be the patient's position, would be likely to attach significance to the risk or cluster of risks in deciding whether or not to forego the proposed therapy.[59]

Factors affecting this materiality determination are the incidence of injury and the degree of harm threatened.[60]

It is important to note that the materiality standard adopted by the court is essentially objective. That is, rather than attempt to assess what the particular patient would consider significant, the court will sanction the physician's conduct if he has provided sufficient information from the standpoint of an "average, reasonable patient."[61] To hold otherwise, declared the court, would impose an undue burden on the physician, for it would force him to second-guess the patient as to the latter's ideas on materiality.

The *Cobbs* case[62] was decided in October 1972, less than six months after *Canterbury*. The plaintiff in the Cobbs case underwent surgery to repair a duodenal ulcer. Two weeks after the surgery (which was uneventful), he was readmitted for removal of his spleen, which had been nicked during the first operation. Subsequently a third operation was necessary because the patient

---

26 A.D.2d 693, 694, 272 N.Y.S.2d 557, 559 (1966), *rev'd in part*, 19 N.Y.2d 407, 227 N.E.2d 269, 280 N.Y.S.2d 373 (1967).

59. 464 F.2d at 787, quoting Waltz and Scheuneman, *Informed Consent to Therapy*, 64 Nw. U. L. Rev. 628, 640 (1970).

60. 464 F.2d at 788. *But see Longmire v. Hoey*, 512 S.W.2d 307, 310 (Tenn. App. 1974), stating that "the serious ·nature of the risk involved is paramount to any percentage figure of occurrence."

The *Canterbury* decision cites the following cases in which materiality was assessed: *Bowers v. Talmage*, 159 So.2d 888 (Fla. Dist. Ct. App. 1963) (3 percent chance of death, paralysis, or other injury—disclosure required); *Scott v. Wilson*, 396 S.W.2d 532 (Tex. Ct. App. 1965), *aff'd*, 412 S.W.2d 299 (Tex. 1967) (1 percent chance of loss of hearing—disclosure required); *Stottlemire v. Cawood*, 213 F.Supp. 897 (D.D.C. 1963), *new trial den.*, 215 F.Supp.266 (D.D.C. 1963) (1/800,000 chance of aplastic anemia—disclosure not required); *Yeates v. Harms*, 193 Kan. 320, 393 P.2d 982 (1964), *on reh.*, 194 Kan. 675, 401 P.2d 659 (1965) (1.5 percent chance of loss of eye—disclosure not required); *Starnes v. Taylor*, 272 N.C. 386, 158 S.E.2d 339 (1968) (1/250 to 1/500 chance of perforation of esophagus—disclosure not required).

61. 464 F.2d at 787. *Accord, Wilkinson v. Vesey*, 110 R.I. 606, 627, 295 A.2d 676, 689 (1972).

62. *Cobbs v. Grant*, 8 C.3d 229 (1972).

developed a severe gastric ulcer, which is a potential complication that is inherent in surgery to relieve a duodenal ulcer. The operation to repair the gastric ulcer was complicated by severe bleeding due to premature absorption of a suture. As the court noted, "The spleen injury, development of the gastric ulcer, gastrectomy, and internal bleeding as a result of the premature absorption of a suture, were all links in a chain of low probability events inherent in the initial operation."[63]

In reviewing prior California law concerning the appropriate standard of care, the California Supreme Court found that in the majority of cases the duty to disclose was measured not by an absolute standard but rather against the practice of a doctor in good standing within the medical community.[64] However, on reviewing the rationale for such a standard, the court found that giving physicians discretion as to disclosure is:

> [I]rreconcilable with the basic right of the patient to make the ultimate informed decision regarding the course of treatment to which he knowledgeably consents to be subjected.[65]

Consequently the court rejected the community standard in favor of the materiality test, as stated in *Canterbury*.[66]

In its discussion of disclosure, the Court appears to distinguish between "common"[67] and "complicated"[68] medical procedures. When "complicated" procedures are contemplated involving a known risk of death or serious bodily harm, the doctor must disclose these risks and explain the possible complications. On the other hand, when a "common" procedure is contemplated, the relatively minor risks involved in such incidents need not be disclosed.[69]

Cobbs and *Canterbury* are the leading cases in the area of informed consent. Since they were decided, the material risk

---

63. *Cobbs v. Grant,* 8 C.3d at 241.
64. Ibid at 241.
65. Ibid at 243.
66. "Thus the test for determining whether a potential peril must be divulged is its materiality to the patient's decision." *Cobbs v. Grant,* 8 C.3d at 245.
67. *E.g.,* the taking of a common blood sample. *Id.* at 224, 502 P.2d at 11, 104 Cal.Rptr. at 515.
68. *E.g.,* surgery to relieve a duodenal ulcer. *Id.*
69. By "minor risks," the court is referring primarily to risks of low incidence even though they may be quite severe. *Id.*

standard has been utilized in a number of other jurisdictions,[70] in some cases with interesting variations. In the case of *Hamilton v. Hardy*,[71] for instance, the court cites *Canterbury et al.* for the principle that expert medical testimony is not necessary to prove the existence and scope of a doctor's duty to warn of material risks. The reason is that "the *duty* to disclose is imposed by law, and does not owe its existence to community medical standards."[72] However, the court goes on to state that once the duty is *prima facie* established, the defendant has the burden of introducing evidence of the extent to which his nondisclosure "complied with community standards."[73] In effect, the *Hamilton* court seems to have retained the professional standard, albeit shifting the burden of proof as to compliance to the defendant.[74]

The trend toward the adoption of a material risk standard has elicited both positive and negative reactions.[75] On the one hand, the standard has been criticized as discouraging patient submission to needed surgery and as imposing an inefficient burden on

---

70. *See Sard v. Hardy*, 379 A.2d 1014 (Ct. of App. of Md., 1977); *Goodwin v. Aetna Cas. & Sur. Co.*, 294 So.2d 618 (La. Ct. of App., 1974); *Zeleznik v. Jewish Chronic Disease Hospital*, 47 A.D.2d 199, 366 N.Y.S.2d 163 (1975); *Congrove v. Holmes*, 37 Ohio Misc. 95, 295, 308 N.E.2d 765 (1973); *Holland v. Sisters of Saint Joseph of Peace*, 270 Or. 129, 522 P.2d 208 (1974); *Cooper v. Roberts*, 220 Pa. Super. Ct. 260, 286 A.2d 647 (1971); *Wilkinson v. Vesey*, 110 R.I. 606, 295 A.2d 676 (1972); *Longmire v. Hoey*, 512 S.W.2d 307 (Tenn. App. 1974); *Small v. Gifford Memorial Hospital*, 133 Vt. 552, 349 A.2d 703 (1975); *Miller v. Kennedy*, 11 Wash. App. 272, 522 P.2d 852 (1974), *aff'd per curiam*, 85 Wash.2d 151, 530 P.2d 334 (1975); *Scaria v. St. Paul Fire & Marine Insurance Co.*, 68 Wis.2d 1, 227 N.W.2d 647 (1975).

71. 549 P.2d 1099 (Colo. App. 1976).

72. *Id.* at 1104-1105.

73. *Id.* at 1105.

74. The burden of persuasion as to the adequacy of disclosure is typically assigned to the plaintiff. *See, e.g., Miller v. Kennedy*, 11 Wash. App. 272, 283, 522 P.2d 852, 861 (1974):

> The burden of proving that a physician failed to inform the plaintiff-patient of the available courses of treatment or failed to warn of the consequential hazards of each choice of treatment is on the plaintiff. It is the plaintiff who must initially establish the existence of the elements of an action based on the informed consent doctrine, i.e., the existence of a material risk unknown to the patient, the failure to disclose it, that the patient would have chosen a different course if the risk had been disclosed and resulting injury.

75. *See* Comment, *Informed Consent: A New Standard for Texas*, 8 St. Mary's L. J. 499 (1976).

the physician.[76] On the other hand, the standard has been praised for producing a better rapport between physicians and patients, for inducing more consultations, and for furthering the ideal of full disclosure.

One argument asserted in support of the material risk standard is its obviation of the need for expert medical testimony to prove a breach of the disclosure duty.[77] However, expert testimony is still required to show (1) the existence and significance of risks attendant with the operation performed, (2) the existence of alternative methods of treatment, and (3) the fact that the plaintiff's injury was caused by the materialization of an undisclosed risk.[78] Moreover, expert testimony may also be necessary to establish any of the available defenses to nondisclosure;[79] to the extent that the plaintiff has the burden of proving the inapplicability of any of these "defenses," the obligation to produce expert testimony will devolve upon him.

Causation

One of the burdens imposed upon the plaintiff in a negligence action is the requirement that he show causation, also referred to as "proximate causation."[80] This requirement has two components.

First, the plaintiff is required to demonstrate[81] that his injury resulted from a risk that should have been, but was not, dis-

76. *See, e.g., Butler v. Berkeley,* 25 N.C. App. 325, 342, 213 S.E.2d 571, 581-82 (1975):

> To adopt the minority rule of *Canterbury* would result in requiring every doctor to spend much unnecessary time in going over with every patient every possible effect of any proposed treatment. The doctor should not have to practice his profession with the knowledge that every consultation with every patient with respect to future treatment contains a potential lawsuit and his advice and suggestions must necessarily be phrased with the possible defense of a lawsuit in mind. This would necessarily result in give the best interest of his patient primary importance. We think the majority rule with respect to informed consent is a much more practical one both in application and result.

77. *See, e.g., Getchell v. Mansfield,* 260 Or. 174, 489 P.2d 953 (1971).
78. *See* Note, *Informed Consent Liability,* 26 Drake L. Rev. 696, 710 (1977); Comment, *New Trends in Informed Consent?,* 54 Neb. L. Rev. 66, 90-91 (1975).
79. These are discussed *infra* at the text accompanying notes 86-111.
80. *See, e.g.,* Meisel, *supra* note 55 at 107-113.
81. The plaintiff has the burden of proof on the causation issue. *E.g., Shetter v. Rochelle,* 2 Ariz. App. 358, 367, 409 P.2d 74, 83 (1965), *mod.,* 2 Ariz. App. 607, 411 P.2d 45 (1966).

closed.[82] Second, the plaintiff must prove that "but for" the failure to disclose, he would not have submitted to the operation:

> Under malpractice theories, there would be no damage proximately resulting from the failure to disclose unless the plaintiff would *not* have had the operation *if the disclosures had been made.* This is an application of the fundamental "but for" rule which comes as close to being of the essence of the proximate cause doctrine as any concept.[83]

Unless the plaintiff succeeds in establishing both components of causation, he will be denied recovery for negligence *even though he has shown a breach of the duty to disclose.*

The second component—i.e., the "but for" requirement—has been the subject of considerable judicial attention. Traditionally, courts appear to have utilized a "subjective" test on this issue; that is, they attempt to ascertain whether the particular plaintiff would have consented to the operation if the risks and alternatives had been properly disclosed.[84] Modern decisions, however, look instead at what a reasonable person in the patient's position would have decided given adequate disclosure.[85] A more detailed description of this "objective" standard, together with the rationale for its adoption, is provided by the following passage from *Canterbury v. Spence:*[86]

> In our view, this [subjective] method of dealing with the issue on causation comes in second-best. It places the physician in jeopardy of the patient's hindsight and bitterness. It places the factfinder

---

82. *See, e.g., Downer v. Veilleux,* 322 A.2d 82, 92 (Me. 1974):
    Proof of proximate cause in [negligence] cases requires, initially, a showing that the unrevealed risk which should have been made known has materialized.
83. *Shetter v. Rochelle,* 2 Ariz. App. 358, 367, 409 P.2d 74, 83 (1965), *mod.,* 2 Ariz. App. 607, 411 P.2d 45 (1966) (citations omitted).
84. *See, e.g., Wilkinson v. Vesey,* 110 R.I. 606, 629, 295 A.2d 676, 690 (1972); *Poulin v. Zartman,* 542 P.2d 271, 275 (Alaska 1975).
85. *See Sard v. Hardy,* 379 A.2d 1014 (Ct. of App. of Md., 1977); *Cobbs v. Grant,* 8 Cal.3d 229, 245, 502 P.2d 1, 11, 104 Cal. Rptr. 505, 515 (1972); *Riedinger v. Colburn,* 361 F.Supp. 1073; 1078 (D. Idaho 1973); *Funke v. Fieldman,* 212 Kan. 524, 537, 512 P.2d 539, 550 (1973); *Fogal v. Genesee Hospital,* 41 A.D.2d 468, 474, 344 N.Y.S.2d 552, 560 (1973); *Cooper v. Roberts,* 220 Pa. Super. Ct. 260, 267-268, 286 A.2d 647, 650-51 (1971); *Karp v. Cooley,* 493 F.2d 408, 422 (5th Cir.) (applying Texas law), *cert. den.,* 419 U.S. 845 (1974); *Small v. Gifford Memorial Hospital,* 133 Vt. 552, 558, 349 A.2d 703, 707 (1975); *Holt v. Nelson,* 11 Wash. App. 230, 236-237, 523 P.2d 211, 216 (1974); *Trogun v. Fruchtman,* 58 Wis.2d 569, 603, 207 N.W.2d 297, 315 (1973).
86. 464 F.2d 772, 790-91 (D.C. Cir. 1972).

in the position of deciding whether a speculative answer to a hypothetical question is to be credited. It calls for a subjective determination solely on testimony of a patient-witness shadowed by the occurrence of the undisclosed risk.

Better it is we believe, to resolve the causality issue on an objective basis: in terms of what a prudent person in the patient's position would have decided if suitably informed of all perils bearing significance. If adequate disclosure could reasonably be expected to have caused that person to decline the treatment because of the revelation of the kind of risk or danger that resulted in harm, causation is shown, but otherwise not. The patient's testimony is relevant on that score, of course, but it would not threaten to dominate the findings. And since that testimony would probably be appraised congruently with the factfinder's belief in its reasonableness, the case for a wholly objective standard for passing on causation is strengthened. Such a standard would in any event ease the factfinding process and better assure the truth as its product. [Footnotes omitted]

In a recent case, the Supreme Court of Massachusetts suggested that both a subjective *and* an objective test should be applied, i.e., that a plaintiff must be able to show not only that he or she would have refused the operation, but also that any reasonable person would have refused it. In denying plaintiff's motion for summary judgment the Court acknowledged the credibility problem inherent in the use of the subjective standard. The plaintiff had sworn an affidavit stating that had she been told of the risk of injury, she "would not have then, under those circumstances, consented to the operative procedure." However, the Court stated that her "bare" assertion that she would have declined the operation "did not carry its own passport of convincingness, despite the sincerity with which she might put it forward long after the event."[87]

Although the objective test has been widely accepted in recent years,[88] it has been strongly criticized by some commentators.[89] The crux of this disapproval has been that an objective standard

---

87. *Schroeder v. Lawrence,* 77 Mass. Adv. Sheet 286, 357 N.E. 2d 1301, 1303 (1977).

88. Indeed, it should be noted that those decisions that seem to use a subjective standard do so without explicitly rejecting an objective standard. Typical of these cases is *Wilkinson v. Vesey,* 110 R.I. 606, 629, 295 A.2d 676, 690 (1972), wherein the court merely states that "the plaintiff must prove that if he had been informed of the material risk, he would not have consented to the procedure. . . ." In essence, one gets the feeling that what appears to be the adoption of a subjective

is inconsistent with the patient's right of self-determination by effectively denying his right to act in what society would consider an unreasonable manner. Certain critics have also suggested that the objective standard unfairly inhibits the plaintiff's chances of recovery. A recent case from the Supreme Court of Maryland, however, demonstrates that a plaintiff may sometimes recover under an objective standard, where he would not have prevailed if a subjective standard had been applied.[90]

Exceptions to the Duty To Disclose

A number of exceptions or defenses to the basic disclosure rule can be gleaned from the multitude of informed consent decisions. To be sure, many of the cases refer to only a few, if any, of these exceptions. Nevertheless, there does seem to be a general consensus among the members of the judiciary as to their validity and applicability, whether it be in the context of a negligence or battery action.

One factor that is often termed an "exception" to disclosure relates to the substantiality of the disclosed risk. In particular, courts have stated that disclosure of minor or remote risks need not ordinarily be made.[91] However, to the extent that the jurisdiction in question employs a material risk-negligence standard, this "exception" may properly be viewed as part of that standard: "minor risk" and "immaterial risk" are essentially synonymous.[92]

Most of the remaining exceptions to the informed consent requirement are relatively straightforward and need no lengthy

test in a particular case may in fact be nothing more than general statements made without thought as to their ramifications.

89. *See, e.g.,* Meisel, *supra* note 55 at 111-12; Note, *Informed Consent Liability,* 26 Drake L. Rev. 696, 712-14 (1977).

90. *In Sard v. Hardy,* 379 A.2d, 1014 (1977), the plaintiff underwent a tubal ligation and later became pregnant. Her physician had failed to discuss the alternative sterilization techniques that were more efficient. The Court held that if the proper information had been given, a reasonable person in the plaintiff's position might not have consented to the procedure that was performed, stating, "The failure on the part of appellant to testify that she would have not consented in the face of a full disclosure is not fatal to her claim." (379 A.2d at 1027).

91. *See* notes 56 and 65, *supra.*

92. In *Holt v. Nelson,* 11 Wash. App. 230, 241, 523 P.2d 211, 219 (1974), the court includes the following as an "exception" to the informed consent rule: "A physician need not disclose risks which have no apparent materiality or relationship to the patient's decision."

exposition. Thus, a physician is not legally obligated to disclose a particular risk if (1) it can be shown that the patient was actually aware of the risk,[93] (2) the existence of the risk was a matter of common knowledge, so that awareness may fairly be imputed to the patient,[94] (3) the risk was not generally known to the medical community at the time the operation was performed,[95] (4) the risk exists only when the operation is improperly performed,[96] or (5) the patient has requested that he not be informed.[97]

Another defense to the informed consent requirement is the existence of a medical emergency.[98] An emergency is deemed to exist when "the patient is unconscious or otherwise incapable of consenting, and harm from a failure to treat is imminent and outweighs any harm threatened by the proposed treatment."[99] In such a situation, consent to the treatment will be implied as a matter of law.[100]

In a dictum, one court has stated that even if an emergency situation does exist, the physician should attempt to secure a

---

93. *Canterbury v. Spence,* 464 F.2d 772, 788 (D.C. Cir. 1972).

94. *See, e.g., Wilkinson v. Vesey,* 110 R.I. 606, 627, 295 A.2d 676, 689 (1972). To succeed in this defense, the physician must show that his assumption about the patient's knowledge was valid in light of a reasonable patient, taking into account the particular patient's circumstances. *See* Comment, *A Doctor's Duty to Inform—Holland v. Sisters of Saint Joseph of Peace,* 1974 Utah L. Rev. 851.

95. *E.g., Trogun v. Fruchtman,* 58 Wis.2d 569, 604, 207 N.W.2d 297, 315 (1973) (risk of drug's side effect was not known to physicians in the Milwaukee area at the time the drug was administered).

96. *Mull v. Emory University,* 114 Ga. App. 63, 66, 150 S.E.2d 276, 292 (1966); *Mallett v. Pirkey,* 171 Colo. 271, 281, 466 P.2d 466, 470 (1970). A related doctrine is that risks associated with an operation based on a mistaken diagnosis need not be disclosed. *Block v. McVay,* 80 S.D. 460, 477, 126 N.W.2d 808, 812 (1964).

97. *Cobbs v. Grant,* 8 Cal. 3d 229, 245, 502 P.2d 1, 12 104 Cal.Rptr. 505, 516, (1972). In this situation, it is recommended that the physician obtain a signed waiver of disclosure from the patient. *See* Alfidi, *Controversy, Alternatives, and Decisions in Complying with the Legal Doctrine of Informed Consent,* 114 Radiology 231, 233-34 (1975).

98. As one commentator has observed, most of the cases that cite this defense do so in a negative fashion; *i.e.,* the court will state that no emergency existed to support its finding that there was a duty to disclose. *See* Plante, *An Analysis of "Informed Consent,"* 36 Fordham L. Rev. 639, 653-54 (1968).

99. *Canterbury v. Spence,* 464 F.2d 772, 788 (D.C. Cir. 1972).

100. *See Cobbs v. Grant,* 8 Cal.3d 229, 243-244, 502 P.2d 1, 10 104 Cal. Rptr. 505, 514, (1972).

relative's consent to the treatment.[101] However, as another court has observed, this precept evidently supposes that the relative has the legal authority to withhold consent on behalf of the patient.[102] Although such may be the case if the patient is a minor or incompetent, it is surely not the case for a competent adult.[103]

The defense to disclosure that has gained the most attention, both in the judicial decisions and the informed consent literature, is the "therapeutic privilege." The essence of this doctrine is that a physician may be privileged to withhold material information from his patient if disclosure would cause the patient's physical or mental condition to deteriorate.[104] Although the origin of the therapeutic privilege is unclear,[105] its modern development may be attributed to the following language from the 1957 case of *Salgo v. Leland Stanford Jr. University Board of Trustees:*[106]

> At the same time, the physician must place the welfare of his patient above all else and this very fact places him in a position in which he sometimes must choose between two alternative courses of action. One is to explain to the patient every risk attendant upon any surgical procedure or operation, no matter how remote; this may well result in alarming a patient who is already unduly apprehensive and who may as a result refuse to undertake surgery in which there is in fact minimal risk; it may also result in actually increasing the risks by reason of the physiological results of the apprehension itself. The other is to recognize that each patient presents a separate problem, that the patient's mental and emotional condition is important and in certain cases may be crucial, and that in discussing the element of risk a certain amount of discretion must be employed consistent with the full disclosure of facts necessary to an informed consent.

As the foregoing quotation indicates, the therapeutic privilege is a product of the notion that the doctor's primary duty is to serve the best interests of his patient.[107] In fact, it is conceivable

---

101. *Canterbury v. Spence,* 464 F.2d 772, 789 (D.C. Cir. 1972).

102. *Nishi v. Hartwell,* 52 Haw. 188, 198-199, 473 P.2d 116, 122 (1970).

103. *Id.*

104. *E.g., Wilkinson v. Vesey,* 110 R.I. 606, 628, 295 A.2d 676, 689 (1972); *Cobbs v. Grant,* 8 Cal.3d 229, 246, 502 P.2d 1, 12, 104 Cal.Rptr. 505, 516 (1972).

105. *See* Meisel, *supra* note 55 at 99, n. 140.

106. 154 Cal. App.2d 560, 578, 317 P.2d 170, 181 (1957).

107. *See, e.g., Watson v. Clutts,* 262 N.C. 153, 159 136 S.E.2d 617, 621 (1964):

that under extreme circumstances, a disclosure made to a particularly sensitive patient might result in liability for emotional distress.[108]

While the existence of a therapeutic privilege does appear to be accepted in virtually all jurisdictions, the standard by which the exercise of the privilege should be judged has not been satisfactorily determined. In particular, it is not clear whether the validity of withholding information is to be a function of customary medical practice, or whether a "lay"[109] standard is to be employed.[110]

Similarly, the circumstances that would justify nondisclosure have been described only in a general manner by the courts. For example, it has been held that the therapeutic privilege will apply where disclosure would "unduly agitate or undermine an unstable patient,"[111] so seriously upset the patient that the patient would not have been able to dispassionately weigh the risks of refusing

---

> Difficulty arises in attempting to state any hard and fast rule as to the extent of the disclosure required. The doctor's primary duty is to do what is best for the patient. Any conflict between this duty and that of a frightening disclosure ordinarily should be resolved in favor of the primary duty.

108. *Cf. Ferrara v. Galluchio,* 5 N.Y.2d 16, 152 N.E.2d 249, 176 N.Y.S.2d 996 (1958) (physician who performed radiation therapy liable for patient's "cancerophobia" following cancer warning from another doctor); *Williams v. Menehan,* 191 Kan. 6, 8, 379 P.2d 292, 294 (1963) ("a complete disclosure . . . could so alarm the patient that it would, in fact, constitute bad medical practice").

109. A lay standard is one that permits a jury to make its own assessment of reasonableness.

110. The confusion is not helped by statements such as the following from *Cobbs v. Grant,* 8 Cal.3d 229, 246, 502 P.2d 1, 12, 104 Cal.Rptr. 505, 516, (1972):

> A disclosure need not be made beyond that required *within the medical community* when a doctor can prove by a preponderance of the evidence he relied upon facts which would demonstrate to a *reasonable man* the disclosure would have so seriously upset the patient that the patient would not have been able to dispassionately weigh the risks of refusing to undergo the recommended treatment. (Emphasis added)

One commentator has stated that this quotation may plausibly be interpreted as imposing a professional test with respect to the *content* of information that may be withheld, but creating a lay standard as to the propriety of invoking the privilege. *See* Meisel, *supra* note 55 at 103, note 151. However, this explanation ignores the fact that the propriety of invoking the privilege depends upon the content of the information withheld.

111. *Wilkinson v. Vesey,* 110 R.I. 606, 628, 295 A.2d 676, 689 (1972).

to undergo the recommended treatment,"[112] or "foreclose a rational decision, or complicate or hinder the treatment, or perhaps even pose psychological damage to the patient."[113] The effect of these broad statements is to give the physician considerable latitude for invoking the privilege. The only obvious circumscription on this discretion is that the physician should not withhold information merely because divulgence might "prompt the patient to forego therapy the physician feels the patient really needs."[114]

A final aspect of the therapeutic privilege concerns the burden of proving its applicability. To the extent that the privilege is viewed as an affirmative defense, it would follow that the burden would rest with the defendant physician.[115] On the other hand, the therapeutic privilege may be deemed an integral part of the basic scope-of-disclosure issue, thereby imposing on the plaintiff the burden of showing its inapplicability.

As yet, there has not been adequate judicial examination of this issue. Although some courts have declared that the defendant has the burden of coming forward with evidence regarding the therapeutic privilege,[116] the responsibility for the ultimate burden of persuasion remains unresolved. This, as well as many of the other issues described above, await further judicial clarification.

There is, however, a significant trend toward codification of informed consent law. Many states have already passed informed consent statutes and in other states, there are bills on this subject now pending before the legislature. To the extent that this trend continues, the rapid evolution of the law in this area will be slowed if not stopped, and the courts will be more concerned with statutory interpretation and less with the social benefits and desirability of physician-patient communication.

---

112. *Cobbs v. Grant,* 8 Cal.3d 229, 246, 502 P.2d 1, 12, 104 Cal.Rptr. 505, 516, (1972).

113. *Canterbury v. Spence,* 464 F.2d 772, 789 (D.C. Cir. 1972).

114. *Id.*

115. *See Miller v. Kennedy,* 11 Wash. App. 272, 283-284, 522 P.2d 852, 861 (1974): "The burden of proving a defense when failure to disclose has been established is on the doctor."

116. *E.g., Canterbury v. Spence,* 464 F.2d 772, 791 (D.C. Cir. 1972); *Cobbs v. Grant,* 8 Cal.3d 229, 245, 502 P.2d 1, 12, 104 Cal.Rptr. 505, 516, (1972); *Trogun v. Fruchtman,* 58 Wis.2d 569, 604, 207 N.W.2d 297, 315 (1973).

chapter 4

legislation concerning
informed consent

At least 23 states have statutes that deal directly with informed consent to medical treatment.[1] The vast majority of these laws were enacted in 1975 and 1976 during the "malpractice crisis." Some appear clearly intended to restrict the ability of

---

1. They are:

    Alaska (Alaska Stat. §09.55.556 [Supp. 1977]);
    Delaware (Del. Code Tit. 18, §6852 [1976]);
    Florida (Fla. Stat. §768.132 [1975]);
    Hawaii (1976 Haw. Sess. Laws Act. 219);
    Idaho (Idaho Code §39-4304 [Supp. 1976]);
    Iowa (Iowa Code Ann. §147.137 [Supp. 1977]);
    Kentucky (Ky. Rev. Stat. Ann. §304.40-320 [Supp. 1976]);
    Louisiana (La. Rev. Stat. Ann. §1299.39 [West, 1977]);
    Maine (Me. Rev. Stat. Tit. 24, §2905 [Cum. Supp. 1977]);
    Nebraska (Neb. Rev. Stat. §44-2816 [Cum. Supp. 1976]);
    Nevada (Nev. Rev. Stat. §41A.100 [1975]);
    New Hampshire (1977 N.H. Laws, Ch. 417);
    New York (N.Y. Pub. Health §2805-d [McKinney Supp. 1976]);
    North Carolina (N.C. Gen. Stat. §90-21.11 [Supp. 1976]);
    Ohio (Ohio Rev. Code Ann. §2317.54, as amended AM. H.B.
      No. 213, eff. Nov. 24, 1977);
    Oregon (1977 Or. Laws, Ch. 657);
    Pennsylvania (Pa. Stat. Ann. Tit. 40, §1301.103 [Supp. 1977]);
    Rhode Island (R.I. Gen. Laws, §9-19-32 [Supp. 1976]);
    Tennessee (Tenn. Code Ann. §23-3414 [Supp. 1976]);
    Texas (1977 Texas Sess. Law Serv., Ch. 817);

plaintiffs to recover in claims based on informed consent;[2] in others the legislature's intent may simply have been to deal with conflicting court decisions, or to prevent a feared judicial expansion of plaintiff's right to recover in medical malpractice actions.

With the exception of Rhode Island,[3] the states that have enacted informed consent statutes have followed two basic approaches. The first, or evidentiary approach, is to list the types of information that a health care provider must give a patient concerning proposed treatment, and then to provide that a signed document attesting that the information has been given constitutes "prima facie" or "conclusive" evidence that an informed consent to treatment has been given. The second, or cause-of-action approach, lists the elements of a cause of action based on lack of informed consent, and the possible defenses to such a claim. The discussion below compares the two general approaches and discusses the relative advantages of each.

The Evidentiary Approach

The evidentiary approach, in its simplest form, is illustrated by the Iowa statute, which states:

A consent in writing to any medical or surgical procedure or course of procedures in patient care which meets the requirements of this section shall create a presumption that informed consent was given. A consent in writing meets the requirements of this section if it:

1. Sets forth in general terms the nature and purpose of the procedure or procedures, together with the known risks, if any, of death, brain damage, quadriplegia, paraplegia, the loss or loss of function of any organ or limb, or disfiguring scars associated with such procedure or procedures, with the probability of each such risk if reasonably determinable.

Utah (Utah Code Ann. §78-14-5 [1977]);

Vermont (Vt. Stat. Ann. Tit. 12, §1908 [Supp. 1977]);

Washington (Wash. Rev. Code Ann. §7.70.050 [Supp. 1976]).

Colorado enacted an informed consent law in 1976 but repealed it in 1977. (See note 36.) Mississippi, Georgia, Arkansas, and Missouri have medical consent laws but no provisions relating to "informed" consent.

2. See, e.g., New York's informed consent statute (N.Y. Pub. Health §2805-d [1976]), which states that the right to recover for medical malpractice based on a lack of informed consent is limited to certain fact situations, and which provides very liberal defenses.

3. Rhode Island's informed consent statute is discussed in the section on Evidence and Procedure, page 55.

2. Acknowledges that the disclosure of that information has been made and that all questions asked about the procedure or procedures have been answered in a satisfactory manner.

3. Is signed by the patient for whom the procedure is to be performed, or if the patient for any reason lacks legal capacity to consent, is signed by a person who has legal authority to consent on behalf of that patient in those circumstances.[4]

The statute requires that each patient be given a bare minimum of information. It does not, for instance, require the physician to inform the patient of alternative treatments or procedures. The only risks that must be disclosed are those of death, brain damage, quadriplegia, paraplegia, loss or loss of function of any organ or limb, and disfiguring scars. The statute does not require medical or expert testimony on any subject, nor does it make reference to burdens of proof, defenses, or an individual's capacity to give an informed consent.

The Ohio informed consent law also follows the evidentiary approach, and as initially adopted (in 1976), it also required the physician to disclose only certain types of risks: namely, death, brain damage, quadriplegia, paraplegia, loss of an organ or limb, loss of function of a limb or organ, or disfiguring scars. A subsequent amendment, however, deleted the list of specific risks and requires, instead, the disclosure of all risks that are "reasonably known."[5] The Ohio law also requires that the person signing the consent be legally competent or that the consent be signed "by a person who has legal capacity to consent on behalf of such patient in such circumstances."[6] If a written form fulfills these requirements, it is

> presumed to be valid and effective, in the absence of proof by a preponderance of the evidence that the person who sought such consent was not acting in good faith, or that the execution of the consent was induced by fraudulent misrepresentation of material facts, or that the person executing the consent was not able to communicate effectively in spoken and written English or other language in which the consent is written.[7]

4. Iowa Code Ann. §147.137 (Supp. 1977).

5. Ohio Rev. Code Ann. §2317.54(A) (1976), as amended Am. H.B. No. 213, effective Nov. 24, 1977.

6. Ibid., §2317.54(C).

7. Ibid., §2317.54. The emphasis in most informed consent statutes is on the nature of information that must be given and not on the ability of the patient to comprehend. See Evidence of Comprehension, page 52.

The Ohio statute is exceptional in providing that a consent administered in English is not effective if the individual consenting cannot communicate in that language.

Other statutes that follow the Iowa-Ohio model are Idaho,[8] Louisiana,[9] and Nevada.[10]

The Cause-of-Action, or Code-Type, Approach

The simplest version of the cause-of-action approach is a Delaware statute, which reads:

(a) No recovery of damages based upon a lack of informed consent shall be allowed in any action for malpractice unless:

(1) The injury alleged involved a nonemergency treatment, procedure or surgery; and

(2) The injured party proved by a preponderance of evidence that the health care provider did not supply information regarding such treatment, procedure or surgery to the extent customarily given to patients, or other persons authorized to give consent for patients, by other licensed health care providers with similar training and/or experience in the same or similar health care communities as that of the defendant at the time of the treatment, procedure or surgery.

(b) In any action for malpractice, in addition to other defenses provided by law, it shall be a defense to any allegation that such health care provider treated, examined or otherwise rendered professional care to an injured party without his or her informed consent that:

(1) A person of ordinary intelligence and awareness in a position similar to that of the injured party could reasonably be expected to appreciate and comprehend hazards inherent in such treatment;

(2) The injured party assured the health care provider he or she would undergo the treatment regardless of the risk involved or that he or she did not want to be given the information or any part thereof to which he or she could otherwise be entitled; or

(3) It was reasonable for the health care provider to limit the extent of his or her disclosures of the risks of the treatment, procedure or surgery to the injured party because further disclosure could be expected to affect, adversely and substantially, the injured party's condition, or the outcome of the treatment, procedure or surgery.[11]

---

8. Idaho Code §39-4304 (Supp. 1976).

9. La. Rev. Stat. Ann. §1299.39 (West) (1977).

10. Nev. Rev. Stat. §41A.100 (1975).

11. Del. Code Ann. Tit. 18, §6852 (1976).

This statute, in very few words, establishes the elements of the cause of action based on lack of informed consent; establishes that the duty to disclose is governed by the "professional," or "community" standard; and provides three significant defenses to such a claim. The statute places on the plaintiff the burden of showing the type of information that must be disclosed and the defendant's failure to disclose that information. Perhaps surprisingly, the statute does not include causation as an element of the cause of action; that is, the plaintiff does not have to prove that if a reasonable prudent person had been given the information, he would have refused the treatment that caused the injury.

Alaska's law is similar to the Delaware statute except that it does require a showing of causation:

> (a) A health care provider is liable for failure to obtain the informed consent of a patient if the claimant establishes by a preponderance of the evidence that the provider has failed to inform the patient of the common risks and reasonable alternatives to the proposed treatment or procedure, *and that but for that failure the claimant would not have consented to the proposed treatment or procedure.* (Emphasis added)[12]

The Nebraska law is similar to Alaska's in that it defines the scope of disclosure by a community standard and requires the plaintiff to establish by a preponderance of the evidence that "a reasonably prudent person in the plaintiff's position would not have undergone the treatment had he been properly informed, and that the lack of informed consent was the proximate cause of the injury and damages claimed."[13] Vermont and New Hampshire have similar laws.[14] A statute enacted in Tennessee[15] is similar in substance though quite different in form; it provides the elements of any "malpractice" cause of action, establishes a community standard for the duty of care; and states that the plaintiff has the burden of proving the defendant's negligence by the preponderance of the evidence. The statute then provides:

> Proving inadequacy of consent.—In a malpractice action the plaintiff shall prove by evidence as required by §23-3414(b) that the defendant did not supply appropriate information to the patient in obtaining his informed consent (to the procedure out

---

12. Alaska Stat. §09.55.556 (Supp. 1977).

13. Neb. Rev. Stat. §44-2816 (Cum. Supp. 1976).

14. Vt. Stat. Ann. Tit. 12, §1908, 1909 (1977); 1977 N.H. Laws, Ch. 417.

15. Tenn. Code Ann. §23-3414 (Supp. 1976).

of which plaintiff's claim allegedly arose) in accordance with the recognized standard of acceptable professional practice in the profession and in the specialty, if any, that the defendant practices in the community in which he practices and in similar communities.[16]

The statutes discussed above are similar in that they follow a code-type approach *and* they adopt the community standard with respect to the scope of disclosure. The state of Utah, on the other hand, while adopting the code-type of approach, does not measure the duty to disclose by a community standard; instead it requires the physician to provide his patient with information concerning "serious and substantial risks."[17]

Washington[18] combines both the cause-of-action and the evidentiary approach in one statute by first establishing the elements of the cause of action, allocating the burden of proof and listing defenses, and then providing that a consent form, signed by the patient, which meets standards detailed in the statute, shall constitute prima facie evidence that the patient gave informed consent to treatment.

Specific Issues

As noted above, most informed consent statutes follow one of two general patterns.[19] The statutes within each group do, however, differ in content with respect to many of the specific issues that have been raised in the litigation of informed consent cases.

Assault Versus Negligence

Some states have attempted to establish by legislation that a claim against a health care provider based on lack of informed consent must be based on negligence rather than battery. Texas, for instance, has a statute that states:

In a suit against a physician or health care provider involving a health care liability claim that is based on the failure of the physician or health care provider to disclose or adequately to disclose the risks and hazards involved in the medical care or

16. Ibid., §23-3414.
17. Utah Code Ann. §78-14-5 (1) (e) (1977).
18. Wash. Rev. Code Ann. §7.70.050 (1976).
19. Four states that have not been discussed above do not fall into either group. They are: New York (N.Y. Pub. Health §2805-d and §4401-a), North Carolina (N.C. Gen. Stat. §90-21.13 [1976]); Florida (Fla. Stat. §768.132 [1975]), and Maine (Me. Rev. Stat. Tit. 24, §2905 [1977]). (The latter three are virtually identical.)

surgical procedure rendered by the physician or health care provider, the only theory on which recovery may be obtained is that of negligence in failing to disclose the risks or hazards that could have influenced a reasonable person in making a decision to give or withhold consent.[20]

Arizona has also enacted legislation that provides that no "medical malpractice" action may be based on assault and battery.[21] The definition of medical malpractice specifically includes claims based on an alleged failure to obtain informed consent.[22] As a result, not only must informed consent laws be brought on a theory of negligence,[23] but also such cases are subject to all the other provisions of Arizona's "medical malpractice law." These include provisions relating to necessary elements of proof,[24] statute of limitations,[25] collateral source evidence,[26] *ad damnum* clauses,[27] and attorney's fees.[28]

Other states have also passed comprehensive medical malpractice laws addressing many of the issues addressed in the Arizona law (above). However, in no other state does the statutory definition of malpractice specifically mention consent. In these states, therefore, it may be argued that a claim based on lack of informed consent is a case of simple battery and not malpractice, and that such claims are therefore exempted from procedural and remedial sections governing "malpractice" actions.

Standard of Disclosure

Most statutes measure the physician's duty to disclose by the so-called "community standard." The Delaware statute, for instance, states:

(a) No recovery of damages based upon a lack of informed consent shall be allowed in any action for malpractice unless:

---

20. 1977 Texas Sess. Law Serv., Ch. 817, §6.02.
21. Ariz. Rev. Stat. § 12-562(B) (1976).
22. Ibid., §12-561(2).
23. *Cathemer v. Hunter,* 358 P.2d 975, 978 n.2 (1976) states: "2. Arizona's Thirty-Second Legislature in its First Special Session in 1976 abrogated a patient's common law right to sue his physician or medical health provider upon the theory of assault and battery."
24. Ibid., §12-563.
25. Ibid., §12-564.
26. Ibid., §12-565.
27. Ibid., §12-566.
28. Ibid., §12-568.

(2) The injured party proved by a preponderance of evidence that the health care provider did not supply information regarding such treatment, procedure or surgery to the extent customarily given to patients, or other persons authorized to give consent for patients, by other licensed health care providers with similar training and/or experience in the same or similar health care communities as that of the defendant at the time of the treatment, procedure or surgery.[29]

This is a strict community standard statute with no minimum disclosure requirements. Conceivably, a physician who disclosed no information whatsoever would meet the statutory standard in Delaware as long as other physicians in the community were similarly silent. Other states have modified the community standard by including a minimum requirement that the patient be informed of medically acceptable alternative procedures and recognized inherent risks.[30] And, as noted above, at least one state has adopted the so-called "materiality" standard, which requires disclosure of "material" facts relating to the proposed treatment.[31]

Texas has developed a very unique approach to standards of disclosure.[32] The Texas statute creates a Medical Disclosure Panel composed of six physicians and three attorneys. The duties of the panel are to determine and list the medical treatments and surgical procedures that do and do not require disclosure of risks and hazards. For those treatments that do require disclosure, the panel "shall establish the degree of disclosure required and the form in which the disclosure will be made."[33] The law provides that a consent that discloses the risks and hazards "in the form and to the degree required by the Panel" shall be "considered effective."[34]

The Texas law establishes an absolute standard; that is, the physician must disclose the exact quantum of information that the panel finds necessary. Failure to do so results in a rebuttable presumption of negligence.[35] Colorado's informed consent law

---

29. Del. Code Ann. Tit. 18, §6852a(2) (1976).
30. See, e.g., Fla. Stat. §768.132(3)(a)(b) (1975).
31. Wash. Rev. Code Ann. §7.70.050(1)(2) (1976).
32. 1977 Texas Sess. Law Serv. Ch. 817, §§6.03-6.07.
33. Ibid., §6.04(b).
34. Ibid., §6.06.
35. Ibid., §6.07(a)(2).

also established an absolute standard of disclosure,[36] but it proved unworkable in practice and the law was repealed within a year of passage.

Causation

As noted above,[37] many informed consent statutes provide that a plaintiff must plead and prove causation, that is, that he would not have consented to the treatment that caused the injury had he been given the necessary information. In one state, causation (or the lack thereof) is made a defense rather than an element of the plaintiff's case.[38] North Carolina and Maine have adopted

---

36. Colo. Rev. Stats. §13-20-301 (1976), repealed H.B. No. 1106, May 27, 1977.

" . . . [A] physician shall provide his patient with sufficient information to enable such patient to give informed consent to the proposed procedure. . . ." §13-20-303(1).

"Sufficient information relating to the proposed procedure" means:

(I) When applicable, the likely result if the patient does not receive the proposed procedure;

(II) When applicable, generally accepted alternative procedures;

(III) The likelihood that death will be a proximate result of the proposed procedures;

(IV) Serious injuries that could result proximately from the proposed procedure and the likelihood of occurrence of each such serious injury;

(V) The likelihood that the proposed procedure will result in no improvement or worsening of the patient's condition.

(b) The information listed in paragraph (a) of this subsection (6) shall be based upon medical knowledge generally available to a reasonable and prudent physician at the time the patient is given said information. [§1320-302(6)(a)]

"Likelihood" means *an approximation of the percentage within two percent of the risk* associated with the procedure, which percentage is either contained in a recognized medical publication or is measured by the experience of the physician out of a substantial number of the same or similar procedures. [§13-20-302(2)] (Emphasis added)

The requirement that risks be disclosed with such exactitude proved unworkable in practice.

37. *Supra,* note 12 and accompanying text.

38. Vt. Code Tit. 12, §1909(c) (1977): "It shall be a defense to any action for medical malpractice based upon an alleged failure to obtain such an informed consent that: . . . (4) A reasonably prudent person in the patient's position would have undergone the treatment or diagnosis if he had been fully informed."

statutes that state that causation must be shown but does not allocate the burden of evidence to either plaintiff or defendant.[39]

Who Can Give Informed Consent

As every hospital attorney knows, a thorny and frequently recurring problem is identifying a person or persons who can consent to medical treatment on behalf of a patient who is incapable of consenting himself. This is not, strictly speaking, a problem of "informed" consent. In fact, the most comprehensive statutes, the Mississippi statute and those modeled on it, deal with the problem of who may consent, but do not deal with the scope and nature of the information to be disclosed.[40] However, some informed consent statutes also deal with the problem. Idaho, for instance, has adopted the following provision:

a. Parent, Spouse, or Guardian: Consent for the furnishing of hospital, medical, dental, or surgical care, treatment, or procedures to any person who is not then capable of giving such consent as provided in this act or who is a minor or incompetent person, may be given or refused by a competent parent, spouse, or legal guardian of such person unless the patient is a competent adult who has refused to give such consent.

b. Competent Relative or Other Person: If no parent, spouse, or legal guardian is readily available to do so, then consent may be given by any competent relative representing himself or herself to be an appropriate, responsible person to act under the circumstances; and, in the case of a never married minor or mentally incompetent person, by any other competent individual representing himself or herself to be responsible for the health care of such person, provided, however, that this subsection shall not be deemed to authorize any person to override the express refusal by a competent adult patient to give such consent himself.[41]

North Carolina and Maine, like Idaho, provide that consent may be given by a patient's spouse or nearest relative.[42]

---

39. N.C. Gen. Stat. §90-21.13(3) (1976); Me. Rev. Stat. Tit. 24, §2905(1) (c) (1977).

40. Miss. Code of 1972 (1966) §41-41-3 et seq. Other statutes based on the Mississippi model include: Ark. Stat. §82-363 and 82-364; La. Rev. Stat. §1299.50 et seq.; Ga. Code Ann. §88-2904 (1976); Mo. Rev. Stat. §431,061. Georgia is the state that has no "informed" consent doctrine (*supra*, chapter 3, note 3).

41. Idaho Code §39-4302 (1976).

42. N.C. Gen. Stat. §90-21.13(a) (1976); Me. Rev. Stat. Tit. 24, §2901 (1977).

Implied Consent

The common-law rule that consent to treatment may be implied in the case of an emergency is recognized explicitly in some statutes and implicitly in others.

The most explicit statement of the common-law rule is the Washington statute:

(4) If a recognized health care emergency exists and the patient is not legally competent to give an informed consent and/or a person legally authorized to consent on behalf of the patient is not readily available, his consent to required treatment will be implied.[43]

Nevada has also codified the common-law implied consent rule,[44] based on statutory recognition of the implication of consent in defined emergencies included in the comprehensive medical consent statutes of Mississippi, Georgia, Arkansas, Louisiana and Missouri.[45]

Kentucky's law provides:

(3) In an emergency situation where consent of the patient cannot reasonably be obtained before providing health care services, there is no requirement that a health care provider obtain a previous consent.[46]

New York,[47] Delaware,[48] and Texas[49] also limit recovery to nonemergency situations.

---

43. Wash. Rev. Code Ann. §7.70.050(4) (1976).

44. Nev. Rev. Stat. §41A.120 (1975):

Consent of Patient: When implied. In addition to the provisions of chapter 129 of NRS and any other instances in which a consent is implied or excused by law, a consent to any medical or surgical procedure will be implied if:

1. In competent medical judgment, the proposed medical or surgical procedure is reasonably necessary and any delay in performing such procedure could reasonably be expected to result in death, disfigurement, impairment of faculties, or serious bodily harm; and

2. A person authorized to consent is not readily available.

It will be noted that even when an emergency exists, consent is necessary if a person "authorized to consent" is "readily" available.

45. See note 40 *supra*.

46. Ky. Rev. Stat. §304.40-320(3) (Supp. 1976). The Pennsylvania statute is similar: "No physician or podiatrist shall be liable for a failure to obtain an informed consent in the event of an emergency which prevents consulting the patient." Pa. Stat. Ann. Tit. 40 §1301.103. The Idaho statute states the same rule, but at greater length. Idaho Code §39-4304 (Supp. 1976).

47. "The right of action to recover for medical malpractice based on lack of informed consent is limited to those cases involving either (a) non-

States that make no explicit provision for emergency situations include: Florida, Iowa, Ohio, Nebraska, North Carolina, Maine, Tennessee, and Utah.

Patient Comprehension

Capacity To Execute

As stated above, many statutes provide that a written and signed consent form, in a prescribed form, is "prima facie," or "conclusive," evidence that a physician has fulfilled his duty to obtain informed consent to treatment. Under common-law principles, a consent, like a contract, is not valid unless the person who executes it is competent. Some statutes state this principle expressly;[50] others do not. A statute such as Nevada's, which provides that a signed consent form is conclusive evidence of consent, without requiring that the patient be competent at the time of signing, is probably invalid.[51]

Evidence of Comprehension

The emphasis in most informed consent statutes is on the type of information that the physician is required to give the patient. In a few states, however, the law includes an explicit or implicit requirement that the information be given in such a way as to be understood by a "reasonable" layman.

Ohio's medical consent law, as discussed previously, provides that a consent is not valid if executed by a person who is not able to "communicate effectively" in the language in which the consent is written.[52] This provision is unique to Ohio. A broader reference

emergency treatment, procedure or surgery. . . ." N.Y. Pub. Health §2805-d(2) (McKinney Supp. 1976).

48. "(a) No recovery of damages based upon a lack of informed consent shall be allowed in any action for malpractice unless: (1) The injury alleged involved a non-emergency treatment, procedure or surgery." Del. Code Ann. Tit. 18, §6852(a) (1976).

49. 1977 Texas Sess. Law Serv. Ch. 817, §6.07(a)(2).

50. "(b) A valid signature is one which is given by a person who under all the surrounding circumstances is mentally and physically competent to give consent." Fla. Stat. §768.132(4)(b) (1975). Other statutes that refer to the patient's mental competence are: N.C. Gen. Stat. §90-21.11 (Supp. 1976); Ohio Rev. Code Ann. §2317.54(c), as amended Am. H.B. No. 213, eff. Nov. 24, 1977.

51. Nev. Rev. Stat. §41A.110 (1975).

52. Ohio Rev. Code Ann. §2317.54, as amended Am. H.B. 213, effective Nov. 24, 1977.

to patient comprehension is found in Vermont's informed consent law:

> (a) For purposes of the section "lack of informed consent" means:
> (1) The failure of the person providing the professional treatment or diagnosis to disclose to the patient such alternatives thereto and the reasonably foreseeable risks and benefits involved as a reasonable medical practitioner under similar circumstances would have disclosed, *in a manner permitting the patient to make a knowledgable evaluation.* (Emphasis added)[53]

Hawaii's statute also suggests that a consent is not valid unless the physician imparts the necessary information in a manner that the patient can understand.[54] Similar references to patient comprehension are found in the Florida law, which states that a claim based on lack of informed consent may not be filed where:

> (b) *A reasonable individual* from the information provided by the physician, osteopath, chiropractor, podiatrist, or dentist under the circumstances, *would have a general understanding* of the procedure and medically acceptable alternative procedures or treatments and substantial risks and hazards inherent in the proposed treatment or procedures . . . Emphasis added)[55]

Kentucky[56] and North Carolina[57] also require that a "reasonable person" would, from the information imparted, "have a general understanding." This language would allow a plaintiff to argue that although a physician disclosed certain information it was not in a form that a reasonable person would understand. Such an argument might well raise an issue of fact sufficient to withstand a motion for summary judgment.

Therapeutic and Other Privileges

The Alaska statute is typical of the "code-type" in providing at least three defenses to a claim based on informed consent, namely: (1) therapeutic privilege, (2) patient waiver, and (3) the information not disclosed was either commonly known or the risk was too remote to require disclosure:

> (b) It is a defense to any action for medical malpractice based upon an alleged failure to obtain informed consent that
> (1) the risk not disclosed is too commonly known or is too remote to require disclosure;

53. Vt. Stat. Ann. Tit. 12, §1909(a) (Supp. 1977).
54. 1976 Haw. Sess. Laws, §3(c).
55. Fla. Stat. §768.132(b) (1975).
56. Ky. Rev. Stat. §304.40-320(2) (Supp. 1976).
57. N.C. Gen. Stat. §90-21.13(a) (2) (Supp. 1976).

(2) the patient stated to the health care provider that he would undergo the treatment or procedure regardless of the risk involved or that he did not want to be informed of the matters to which he would be entitled to be informed;

(3) under the circumstances consent by or on behalf of the patient was not possible; or

(4) the health care provider after considering all of the attendant facts and circumstances used reasonable discretion as to the manner and extent that the alternatives or risks were disclosed to the patient because he reasonably believed that a full disclosure would have a substantially adverse effect on the patient's condition.[58]

Other statutes that provide as a defense a therapeutic privilege and patient waiver are Delaware,[59] New York,[60] Utah,[61] Vermont,[62] and, in slightly modified form, Pennsylvania.[63] Washington does not provide for a therapeutic privilege or for patient waiver.

Section (b)(1) of the Alaska statute, quoted above, represents one approach to limiting liability in informed consent cases, namely to risks that are not "commonly known" or not "too remote to require disclosure." Other states have adopted slightly different formulae. In Vermont for instance, the statute provides a defense where the risk not disclosed is not "substantial,"[64] whereas the Delaware statute does not mention either the probability or severity of the risk but does allow defendants a defense if:

(1) A person of ordinary intelligence and awareness in a position similar to that of the injured party could reasonably be expected to appreciate and comprehend hazards inherent in such treatment.[65]

Statutes that follow the evidentiary model do not list defenses. Many do provide, however, that only information concerning very serious injuries be given (for example, injuries involving death, paraplegia, and loss of organ or limb). Under such a statute, a

58. Alaska Stat. §09.55.556 (Supp. 1977).
59. Del. Code Ann. Tit. 18, §6852(b) (2;3) (1976).
60. N.Y. Pub. Health §2805-d(4) (d;b) (McKinney Supp. 1976).
61. Utah Code Ann. §78-14-15(2) (c;d) (1977).
62. Vt. Stat. Ann. Tit. 12, §1909(c) (2) and (d) (1977).
63. Pa. Stat. Ann. Tit. 40, §1301.103 (Supp. 1977).
64. Vt. Stat. Ann. Tit. 12, §1909(c) (1) (1977). *See also* Utah Code Ann. §78-14-5(2) (a) (b) (1977).
65. Del. Code Tit. 18, §6852(b) (1) (1976).

common procedure (such as taking a blood sample, or administering an injection of penicillin) that does not involve such potential injuries would not require informed consent.

Evidence and Procedure

As stated above,[66] the scope of disclosure in informed consent cases is measured by a "community" standard in some states, and by a "materiality" standard in others. In "community standard states" expert testimony is always necessary to establish the type of information commonly disclosed by physicians in the community. In states that adopt a "materiality" standard, expert testimony will also be required in most instances, because the plaintiff must prove with respect to a given procedure, what the material risks are, as well as the alternative modes of treatment.

A few states require expert medical testimony by statute. One of these is New York, whose statute states:

> A motion for judgment at the end of the plaintiff's case must be granted as to any cause of action for medical malpractice based solely on lack of informed consent if the plaintiff has failed to adduce expert medical testimony in support of the alleged qualitative insufficiency of the consent.[67]

Vermont also allows a motion for judgment where the plaintiff does not offer expert testimony.[68] In Nevada, there is a statute requiring expert testimony in any case against a "provider of medical care" based on "alleged negligence in the performance of such care."[69] This statute presumably applies to claims based

---

66. *Supra,* Standard of Disclosure, pp. 47-49.
67. N.Y. Civ. Prac. §4401-a (McKinney Supp. 1976).
68. Vt. Stat. Ann. Tit. 12, §1909(e) (1977). *See also* Wash. Rev. Code Ann. §7.70.050(3) (1976): "Material facts under the provisions of this section which must be established by expert testimony shall be . . ."
   The Tennessee statute states: "In a malpractice action the plaintiff shall prove by evidence as required by §23-3414(b) that the defendant did not supply appropriate information to the patient by obtaining his informed consent (to the procedure out of which plaintiff's claim allegedly arose) in accordance with the recognized standard of acceptable professional practice in the profession and in the specialty, if any, that the defendant practices in the community in which he practices and in similar communities." Tenn. Code Ann. §23-3417 (1970). (Section 23-3414(b) states that expert testimony must be given by a physician licensed to practice in Tennessee or in a bordering state and practicing a relevant specialty.)
69. Nev. Rev. Stat. §41A.100 (1975):
   Liability for personal injury or death shall not be imposed upon any provider of medical care based on alleged negligence in the per-

on lack of informed consent, as well as negligent treatment and diagnosis.

Rhode Island has enacted a procedural statute that is unique. The statute states:[70]

> In actions against licensed physicians for malpractice in providing treatment to patients, issues of informed consent or reasonable disclosure of all known material risks by the physician to the patient, shall be initially considered by the court as preliminary questions of fact. Such issues shall be submitted to the jury by the court only in the event that it finds, after weighing the evidence and considering the credibility of the witnesses, that reasonable minds might fairly come to different conclusions in respect to such issues on the basis of the evidence presented and inferences to be drawn therefrom.[70]

One may speculate that the intent of the legislature in enacting this statute was to preclude the jury from considering informed consent claims that are totally without merit but that, by their nature, are not subject to summary judgment.

Conclusion

It is too early to say how informed consent laws will be applied in the courts and what effect, if any, these laws will have on medical practice and on the physician's duty to obtain a document showing informed consent was given. However, in two states, laws concerning informed consent have already been sent back to the legislature for modification due to pressure from the medical community. The Colorado statute was repealed in toto, because its very precise requirements concerning approximation of risks proved impossible to implement in practice.[71] The Ohio statute as originally written included an extremely complex consent form. This form was deleted from the statute, along with the language specifying the exact nature of the risks that must be disclosed.[72]

---

formance of such care unless evidence consisting of expert medical testimony, material from recognized medical texts or treatises or the regulations of the licensed health care facility wherein such alleged negligence occurred is presented to demonstrate the alleged deviation from the accepted standard of care in the specific circumstances of the case and to prove causation of the alleged personal injury or death except . . .

70. R.I. Gen. Laws, §9-19-32 (Supp. 1976).
71. See note 36 supra.
72. See note 5 supra.

The experience in Ohio seems to support the conclusion that it is difficult if not impossible to design a single form that can be used by all physicians to obtain and document informed consent.[73] The Colorado experience also indicates that an overly rigid definition of the scope of disclosure is ill-advised. The Texas experiment represents an extreme attempt at defining the extent of disclosure.

One may hazard a guess that the three statutes cited above represent one response to the demand of physicians, and other providers, for some certainty in the area of informed consent. Physicians, understandably, want a law that clearly defines the extent of their duty to disclose, a law that provides assurance that "If I do this, I can't be sued." One may also, however, hazard a guess that the laws that appear most reassuring are those that are most likely to be liberally "interpreted" by the courts. For instance, we would suspect that a court would "read into" the Nevada statute a requirement that a patient who signs a consent form be competent at the time of signing.

In the following chapter, the authors offer a model statute that adopts the cause-of-action approach and does not rigidly define the scope of disclosure. We believe that this type of statute most closely reflects the consensus of present judicial thinking. Such a statute provides only the most general guidance to health care providers, but it does serve the purpose of codifying current judicial positions and retarding or preventing future judicial expansion of the common law of informed consent.

---

73. See chapter 6 *infra*.

chapter 5

model statute

The following model statute has been developed for purposes of discussion and as an aid to those who are considering legislation in this area. It should be noted, however, that many experts question the need for such legislation and that, although informed consent laws have been passed in a number of states, none of these laws have as yet been tested in the courts.

Model Statute

1 **01—Informed Consent—Elements of Proof**

2   a. In a claim against a health care provider involving an
3 alleged breach of duty by the provider to secure an informed
4 consent from the patient or his representative, the injured
5 party shall prove by a preponderance of the evidence that:

6   i. The health care provider failed to inform the
7   patient or his representative of a material fact
8   or facts relating to the treatment;

9   ii. That the patient or his representative was not
10   informed of nor aware of such material fact or
11   facts;

12   iii. That a reasonably prudent patient under simi-
13   lar circumstances would not have consented to
14   the treatment if informed of such material fact
15   or facts; and

59

16   iv. That the treatment in question proximately
17   caused the injury to the patient.

18   b. Under the provisions of this section, "material fact"
19 means information that a reasonably prudent person in the
20 position of the patient or the patient's representative would
21 deem necessary in deciding whether or not to submit to
22 the proposed treatment.

23   The following material facts must be established by
24 expert medical testimony:

25   i. The nature and character of the treatment pro-
26   posed and administered;

27   ii. The reasonably expected results of the treat-
28   ment proposed and administered;

29   iii. The recognized available alternative methods
30   of treatment; and

31   iv. The significant risks and complications of con-
32   sent to nontreatment, the treatment adminis-
33   tered, and the available alternative forms of
34   treatment, with such significance being deter-
35   mined by taking into account both probability
36   and severity of risks under the circumstances.

37   c. It is a defense to any action against a health care
38 provider based upon an alleged failure to obtain informed
39 consent that:

40   i. The risk not disclosed is so remote as to make
41   disclosure for consent purposes unnecessary
42   under the circumstances;

43   ii. The patient or his representative stated to the
44   health care provider that he would undergo the
45   treatment or procedure regardless of the risk
46   involved or that he did not want to be informed
47   of some or all of the matters to which he would
48   otherwise be entitled to be informed; or

49   iii. The health care provider, after consideration
50   of all reasonably applicable facts and circum-
51   stances, used reasonable discretion as to the
52   manner and extent to which the alternatives,
53   complications, or risks, were disclosed to the
54   patient because the health care provider rea-

55 sonably believed that a full disclosure would
56 have a substantial and adverse effect on the
57 patient's condition.

58 **02—Consent—When Implied**

59 The patient's consent to treatment will be implied if:

60 a. The patient is not legally competent to give an in-
61 formed consent to treatment; and

62 b. In the reasonable opinion of the treating physician,
63 the treatment provided is necessary for the alleviation of
64 severe pain or for the diagnosis and/or treatment of a
65 condition that if not immediately treated could lead to
66 death, disability, serious impairment of health, or substan-
67 tial or inordinate pain.

68 **03—Consent—Who May Give**

69 a. Parent, Spouse, or Guardian: Consent for the furnish-
70 ing of hospital, medical, dental, or surgical care, treatment,
71 or procedures to any adult person who is not then capable
72 of giving such consent may be given or refused by a com-
73 petent spouse, parent, custodian, guardian, or other legal
74 representative of such person. If the patient is a minor,
75 consent may be given or refused by the patient's parent or
76 legal guardian.

77 b. Other Authorized Person: If a patient is not capable
78 of giving an informed consent, and if no person described
79 in the preceding paragraph is readily available to do so,
80 then consent may be given by any competent relative
81 representing himself or herself to be an appropriate, respon-
82 sible person to act under the circumstances.

83 **04—Health Care Provider**

84 a. "Health care provider" means a person, corporation,
85 or institution licensed or certified by the state to provide
86 health care, medical services, nursing services, or other
87 health-related services and includes the officers, employees,
88 and agents thereof lawfully rendering such care or services
89 under the supervision of such person, corporation, or insti-
90 tution in providing such health care services.

91 b. The duty to obtain an informed consent is that of the
92 physician and surgeon, dentist, or podiatrist, or other prac-

93   titioner who orders or prescribes the treatment or who
94   undertakes and administers the treatment in the exercise
95   of independent medical discretion.

96   c. No claim based on the alleged breach of duty to secure
97   an informed consent shall be brought against a health care
98   provider who renders treatment pursuant to the order of
99   another health care provider unless the person or corpora-
100   tion rendering treatment knew, or should have known, that
101   no informed consent had been given.

102   **05—Patient Representative**

103   "Patient representative" means a person authorized by
104   section 03 to give a consent to treatment for another person
105   who is the patient, and any other person so authorized by
106   official appointment or legal or familial relationship to the
107   patient.

108   **06—Treatment**

109   "Treatment" includes diagnostic procedures as well as
110   therapeutic measures.

Discussion

Sources

This statute adopts the cause-of-action rather than the evidentiary approach. In most respects, it follows the decision of the California Supreme Court in *Cobbs v. Grant* (8 Cal.3d 222, [1972]), which is a leading case on informed consent.

Part 01 (Elements of Proof) is based on the Washington statute (Wash. Rev. Code Ann. § 7.70.050 [Supp. 1976]). Part 02 (Consent—When Implied) and Part 03 (Consent—Who May Give) are based on the Idaho statute (Idaho Code § 39-4304 [Supp. 1976]). Part 04 (Health Care Provider) is original.

Evidentiary Problems

A number of states have enacted legislation that provides that an executed document in a given format establishes a presumption (or conclusive presumption) that informed consent has been obtained. There is no such provision in this statute, because in the opinion of the author, the doctor-patient dialog is generally too lengthy to be accurately documented. Moreover, a statute that provides for a conclusive presumption is likely not to be upheld if a judge or jury finds that the document was not reasonably comprehensible by the patient (for example, because in a foreign language or because of technical terminology).

Specific Issues

1. Line 5: The burden of proof is on the injured party.

2. Line 6: The statute requires disclosure of material facts. This is the standard in California, following the decision in *Cobbs v. Grant*, and in Washington, by statute. In many other states the standard of disclosure is the so-called "community standard."

3. Line 18: The definition of material fact follows the opinion in *Cobbs v. Grant*, 8 Cal.3d 243-245 (1972).

4. Lines 31-36: With respect to risks, only those risks that are "serious" are considered material. Minor risks, therefore, are not material and need not be disclosed. *See Cobbs v. Grant:*

> Some courts have spoken of "full disclosure" and others refer to "full and complete" disclosure, but such facile expressions obscure common practicalities. Two qualifications to a requirement of "full disclosure" need little explication. First, the patient's interest in information does not extend to a lengthy polysyllable discourse on all possible complications. A mini-course in medical science is not required; the patient is concerned with the risk of death or bodily harm, and problems of recuperation. Second, there is no physician's duty to discuss the relatively minor risks inherent in common procedures, when it is common knowledge that such risks inherent in the procedure are of very low incidence. (*Cobbs* at 244; citations omitted)

5. Lines 40-42: The defendant may show, as a defense, that the risk that materialized was too remote to require disclosure.

> Whenever appropriate, the court should instruct the jury on the defenses available to a doctor who has failed to make the disclosure required by law. . . . Such a disclosure need not be made if the procedure is simple and the danger remote and commonly appreciated to be remote. (*Cobbs* at 245)

6. Lines 43-48: The patient may waive his right to full disclosure.

> Thus a medical doctor need not make disclosure of risks when a patient requests that he not be so informed. (*Cobbs* at 245)

7. Lines 49-57: There is provision for a therapeutic privilege.

> A disclosure need not be made beyond that required within the medical community when a doctor can prove by a preponderance of the evidence he relied upon facts which would demonstrate to a reasonable man the disclosure would have so seriously upset the patient that the patient would not have been able to dispassionately weigh the risks of refusing to undergo the recommended treatment. (*Cobbs* at 246)

8. Lines 56-67: Consent is implied in an emergency.

9. Lines 68-76: The spouse of an adult incompetent patient is given the authority to consent to treatment. This represents a substantial departure from the common law. Compare with language of statutes cited at note 40 *supra*, chapter 4.

10. Lines 77-82: The authority to consent to treatment is also extended to any "competent relative" who represents himself as an "appropriate responsible person to act under the circumstances."

This provision, adopted from an Idaho statute, provides a partial solution to the problem that commonly develops when a minor is brought for treatment by someone other than a parent.

11. Lines 83-101: The duty to obtain an informed consent is placed on the physician or other practitioner who orders or prescribes the treatment. Other health care providers, including hospitals, cannot be held liable for the physician's failure to obtain an informed consent unless they know or should have known that such consent was not given.

chapter 6

an alternative to legislative reaction: one state's practical response to a judicial position

Prior to the California Supreme Court decision in *Cobbs v. Grant* in October 1972 (see the special report on the case appearing as appendix A, the hospitals and physicians in California had treated the problem of informed consent as an issue of relatively low priority. Other consent issues, such as the right of a minor to execute a consent or the definition of an incompetent, received greater attention and proposed legislative action.

In part, this state of affairs resulted from a dialog between the California Hospital Association (CHA) and the California Medical Association (CMA) in the 1960s relating to the role of hospital personnel in obtaining the execution of medical consent forms for the physician.

When the CHA *Consent Manual* was first drafted in 1954, the then existing standard hospital-surgical consent form was modified to include, in lay language, a specific reference to the procedure to be performed. Prior to that time, hospital consent forms provided that the surgeon could perform any procedure at his sole discretion and the patient was required to sign such a blanket consent as a condition to being admitted to surgery.

It would be nice to say that this action was in anticipation of the whole informed consent problem, but such was not the case. The purpose was to establish an additional check or control over the communication between the surgeon, on the one hand, and the admitting office and the surgery supervisor on the other. The breakdown of this communication link had led to a number of tragic malpractice cases in which the patient had been prepped for the wrong surgery and this error was not caught until it was too late. By describing the procedure on the form, a check was being made to find out if the patient knew what procedure he was going to undertake and create a written record signed by the patient that would act as an additional check on the communication between the physician and the surgery supervisor. There was considerable physician resistance to the change but, with the recounting of a few horror stories about the wrong patient, the wrong leg, the wrong kidney, and so forth, the procedure was accepted.

When litigation about informed consents developed in the rest of the country with increasing frequency, California hospitals received requests from various specialty groups to have the hospital admission office obtain the patient's signature on some written form waiving all of the patient's rights and consenting to any action by the surgeon. The California Hospital Association advised hospitals to reject these forms on the grounds that hospital employees were not competent to explain the procedure to the patients and respond to patients' questions. Only the admitting physician or the surgeon had both the technical knowledge as well as the background of the particular patient's condition with which to respond. The example was given of an admission clerk on her second day of duty covering a Saturday night shift attempting to respond intelligently to a patient's medical questions about a specific medical procedure. When further pressed, the hospital could suggest that, if it were to fully inform the patient of the risks, it would have to include the risks of having selected that particular surgeon based on his track record at the hospital. Pursuant to long-standing relationships with the California Medical Association, all advice given by the hospital association to its members was fully coordinated and cleared with the medical association so that the physicians and hospitals were not giving conflicting advice.

When the Supreme Court published its opinion in *Cobbs v. Grant*, it received widespread publicity in medical publications. As might be expected, the opinion was widely misinterpreted and the reactions within the medical community were very serious. These reactions ranged from a demand for immediate legislation to reverse the decision, on the one hand, to drafts of proposed consent forms so detailed and specific as to frighten an apprehensive patient into complete panic, on the other. There was an immediate demand by physicians that hospital personnel assume responsibility for obtaining patient signatures on a wide variety of forms. Some of these forms were drawn out of a sense of physician frustration at the judiciary's interference with the physician-patient relationship and, as a reaction, the forms were so harsh in their tone and language as to indicate a desire by the physician to punish his patient (who, it was hoped, was either a judge or a lawyer).

Fortunately, calm heads prevailed. There was an immediate communication between the leadership of CMA and CHA, and CMA reaffirmed its advice to its members that an informed consent was a communication between the physician and patient, and no hospital form could substitute. Furthermore, the CMA questioned the efficacy of a signed printed form as the ultimate solution to the problem. Legal counsel for both associations agreed that although *Cobbs v. Grant* created certain problems, fundamentally the decision was well balanced and at least gave the physicians and hospitals some guidelines to follow to minimize potential liability. However, unless sound direction was given to the health care providers and hospitals, serious legal complications would follow from an overreaction.

The CMA immediately created an ad hoc committee with representation from all of the major medical specialties to advise the medical community. Hospital association representatives participated in the committee deliberations. To give the committee sufficient time to perform its role, the CMA issued a report (appendix A), which had a calming effect on the profession.

The ad hoc committee took several months to complete its work. After approving the general content of the report, the committee determined that, not only was it impossible to prepare a single model informed consent form for general use but also the protocol to be followed would vary by medical specialty.

After adopting some general guidelines, each specialty was requested to prepare its own protocol. An example of such protocol is shown in appendix B.

The protocols were to highlight the special matters to be discussed with the patient, the pros and cons of the particular procedure, the alternatives to surgery, and the like. Nearly every protocol pointed out that the use of a printed form signed by the patient was not the only recommended approach, or even the preferred solution. What was emphasized was the critical importance of communication, primarily oral, but also with the use of communication aids, such as slides, pamphlets, audiovisual presentations, and so forth. Above all, it was important for the patient to have an opportunity to ask questions and to affirm that he was satisfied that he was informed regarding the procedure to be undertaken. All protocols gave instructions to the physician on permanently recording the method and content of the communication. The various protocols were printed and distributed to all specialties.

On the hospital side, the CHA accepted responsibility for revising the hospital consent form. It was agreed that the hospital form primarily should serve the purpose of obtaining consent to routine hospital procedures as a protection to the hospital and its personnel and also to act as a final check and reminder to the patient of his right to be informed by his physician. (A copy of this form is attached as appendix C.) Such difficult matters as the responsibility for obtaining the informed consent to anesthesia or emergency room consents were left to the individual medical staffs to resolve through appropriate committee action.

The CMA and CHA then conferred on the issue of whether to propose a legislative solution. The joint conclusion was that a statutory solution would probably create more problems than it would resolve and that they would prefer to rely on the *Cobbs v. Grant* decision guidelines, pending further development. Although there are still many allegations of lack of informed consent in malpractice complaints, the number of adverse judgments on this ground is minimal. This is the result of a strong educational program with both physicians and hospitals. The educational program has emphasized the position that the "informed consent" is nothing more than "good medicine" and is not a conspiracy by the judiciary and the legal profession to impose another intolerable burden on the medical profession. It also points out that the doctrine applies to all of the professions—particularly lawyers.

By and large, the problem of the lack of informed consent has not loomed great in the California pattern of malpractice cases. Defense counsel indicate that they win the cases that they should, but may be forced to settle otherwise defendable cases when there is little or no documentary evidence in the record that the physician has properly filled his role. The courts are sticking to the guidelines of *Cobbs v. Grant* and are not expanding the potential liabilities as originally feared.

Unfortunately, this is not the complete California story on the matter of informed consents. The legislature is now faced with a variety of specific demands for laws or regulations relating to informed consent in specific areas. One example is the recently adopted California Natural Death Act, which has many overtones of the informed consent as related to the right to die with dignity. At the other end of the life spectrum, the State Department of Health is now faced with a very comprehensive set of regulations relating to all elective sterilization procedures, both male and female, under the guise of informed consent. Also, various consumer groups are attempting to implement the social, moral, and ethical concepts of the proponents. A very comprehensive statute has been adopted covering all types of care for the mentally ill and, of course, the matter of informed consent is covered in this sensitive area of health law.

If pressures continue to force piecemeal adoption of informed consent laws, then CHA and CMA may well be forced to reconsider their present position of opposition to an overall legislative intervention.

The California history is typical of the decision-making process that has occurred in many states. As is indicated in chapter 4, various solutions have been followed. The California lesson emphasizes the importance of physician-hospital cooperation on all sensitive patient care issues, regardless of the ultimate course adopted.

special report: some advice on informed consent

As a service to its members, the California Medical Association has pre-pared advice and guidance for physicians on the applications of "informed consent" in light of the recent California Supreme Court ruling on this subject. These questions and answers cover general topics of importance. More specific advice is being prepared by the CMA ad hoc Committee on Informed Consent for distribution at a future date. This report is reprinted with the permission of the California Hospital Association.

Q: **The California Supreme Court recently handed down a very important decision *(Cobbs v. Grant)*, which affects every physician who is actively practicing medicine. We are told it has a significant and immediate effect on the physician's responsibility to obtain a patient's consent before providing medical treatment. Please explain what this decision is all about.**

A: Before discussing the recent decision, it would be useful to understand the origin of the physician's duty in this respect. Under the law, if injury results from physical contact, the injured person has a civil cause of action known as assault and battery. The law recognizes certain defenses, the most common being "consent." If one person consents to the possi-bility that he will be harmed by another, the law will not allow the injured party to complain. This rule applies in the area

71

of medical treatment. In emergencies where it is physically impractical or impossible for the patient to express his consent, the law implies that he has consented. But in non-emergency situations, his consent must be given.

Q: **Physicians have heard over and over again about the doctrine of *"informed* consent." What do the courts really mean when they say that "consent" must be "informed"?**

A: The law recognizes that medicine is a mystery to the average patient, and he might consent to a particular treatment or procedure without really understanding the consequences. When courts say that a patient's consent must be *informed*, the courts are saying that the patient's consent, to be binding, must be made with his eyes open to the consequences. This increasing focus by the courts on the patient's rights may be more readily understood by viewing it as another illustration of the growing trend toward consumerism or consumers' rights.

Q: **Why have the courts singled out physicians in this respect? Is there something peculiar about the patient-physician relationship which makes doctors particularly vulnerable in this area?**

A: Yes. In the *Cobbs v. Grant* decision, the Supreme Court explained and expanded upon the reasons for the doctrine. The Court adopted four basic principles. They are:
1. Patients are generally persons unlearned in the medical sciences.
2. An adult person of sound mind has the right to determine whether or not to submit to lawful medical treatment.
3. The patient's consent to treatment, to be legally effective, must be an informed consent.
4. The patient, being unlearned in medical sciences, has dependence upon and trust in his physician for the information upon which he relies during his decision process. This raises an obligation for the physician that transcends the marketplace.

These basic principles call for a "due care duty" for physicians to explain to patients those facts necessary for the patient to make an informed judgment regarding his consent to medical treatment.

Q: It is apparent that the *patient*, and not the physician, has the legal right to determine whether or not he will undergo a proposed medical procedure. Does this mean that the patient has the right to refuse medical treatment, even that which would be in his best interest, and the physician must abide by that decision?

A: Precisely. For example, the physician may regard a radical mastectomy as the best treatment for the patient's breast cancer. But he must discuss possible alternatives such as a simple mastectomy or radiation therapy. It will be up to the patient to make the final decision.

Q: It is extremely important that physicians know how extensively they must inform the patient. Exactly what are these things which have to be disclosed?

A: The "what" of informed consent basically can be divided into three areas:
1. The physician must describe the proposed treatment in lay terms so that the patient understands the nature of what is proposed. The explanation does not have to constitute a "mini-course" in medicine.
2. The risks of the proposed therapy must be explained.
3. If there are any alternative choices of treatment, those should be disclosed.

Q: Because this doctrine potentially applies to virtually every kind of medical treatment which involves "contacting" the patient in some way, it would also apply to any type of elective major surgery. But what about the prescription or administration of potent drugs or of minor surgical procedures such as the removal of warts and so on?

A: The Court distinguishes between those procedures which it labels "complex" and those which it labels "simple" and "common." For those procedures which are complex (certainly elective surgery and risky diagnostic procedures fall into this category), the physician has a duty to explain the nature of the procedure; any risks, regardless of their likelihood, which could cause serious bodily harm; and the alternative methods of treatment, if any.

As to procedures which are "simple" and "common," the Court states that a physician cannot be expected to explain risks which are commonly understood to be remote. The Court cited a "blood count" as an example. A typical physical examination would probably be another example.

Q: **There are going to be many types of medical treatment which do not fall clearly into either complex or simple procedures. For example, what about the prescription of certain drugs, such as Chloromycetin? These drugs may involve certain risks which, although extremely remote, may cause serious illness or even death.**

A: There is no question but that the decision leaves many questions unanswered. There are going to be gray zones, procedures which defy simple categorization as "complex" or "simple" and "common." The prescription of potent drugs is one such area. The Court appears to say that for drugs whose prescription is relatively common, there is no duty to disclose remote risks. On the other hand, even remote risks must be described if the drug is in the experimental stage, prescribed only rarely, or has been on the market for a relatively short period of time.

Q: **The physician's duty is described as three-pronged: explaining the nature of the treatment, risks, and alternative methods of treatment. Please elaborate on when an explanation of "alternative methods of treatment" is important.**

A: The importance of this statement in the Court's opinion cannot be overemphasized. For example, take the patient who is told he must have a thyroidectomy for his Graves' disease, and then winds up with some inherent complication of the procedure. The physician runs a severe risk of professional liability if he has failed to warn the patient, not only of the risks but also of the alternative treatments, such as radioactive iodine therapy and the use of antithyroid drugs. Furthermore, where surgery is purely elective, the physician must be especially careful to explain alternative treatments and risks.

Q: **What is there about more urgent treatment which places less of a burden on the physician?**

A: The Court does not expressly distinguish between urgent and elective types of treatment, but, in practical terms, there is an important difference. In addition to proof that an informed consent was not obtained, the Court requires that the patient prove that a *"reasonable man"* would have refused treatment, if the essential information had been provided.

Under this rule, a patient is not going to make a convincing case if he merely testifies that he would not have consented had he known certain facts, in the face of strong medical necessity for the treatment given. It is doubtful in such a case that a jury would consider his refusal under those circumstances as "reasonable."

Q: **Nevertheless, wouldn't it appear that the safest practice is to inform all patients routinely?**

A: Undoubtedly this is true. However, in cases where the treatment is urgent, it would appear that the patient is going to have a heavier burden in convincing a jury that a "reasonable man" would have refused if he had known a particular risk or alternative procedure.

On the other hand, for example, take the patient who has low back pains and no neurological changes and is subjected to surgery without explanation of risks or a discussion of conservative and long-term treatment. This patient has a sure-fire case if he winds up with arachnoiditis.

Q: **There is a strong feeling in the medical community that physicians should, in certain situations, be able to withhold certain information without incurring legal liability. What about the gravely ill patient for whom the procedure contemplated by the physician may involve serious risks? The physician might decide not to explain certain risks for fear that such information would hamper the patient's treatment or seriously depress him. Under these circumstances, what is a physician's duty?**

A: This is one of the most important but also one of the most difficult areas in which to advise. The decision appears to state that a physician may make a judgment to withhold information about certain risks if he decides that disclosure would be detrimental to the mental or physical well-being of the patient. However, the Court is careful to point out that the standard to be applied in deciding whether the physician was justified in withholding this information will not be a medical one, but will be a "reasonable man" standard. This means that the jury will decide, without the aid of expert medical testimony, whether the physician was justified in withholding this information. There is no question but that a physician who takes this course increases his malpractice liability risk.

Q: **What is a physician's duty if the patient really doesn't want to hear about details of an operation or its risks?**

A: If the patient, on his own initiative, informs the physician that he does not want to be informed, the physician's duty to inform ceases as of that point. It is imperative, however, that the patient's decision be made freely and not the result of any intimidation on the part of the physician.

Q: **It's one thing to understand the problem and the reasons why it is necessary that physicians obtain an informed consent. But how can physicians prove in court that the consent was an informed consent? Isn't it just his word against the patient's?**

A: This decision makes several things very clear. First, if a physician relies solely on the fact that he had a conversation with the patient and preserves no written evidence of that conversation, he is begging to be held liable for malpractice.

Secondly, the typical standardized hospital consent form is virtually useless as a protection to the physician. There are several reasons for this. The most important is that the typical consent form contains no actual explanation of the treatment or of the risks, so it conveys none of the essential information to the patient.

Therefore, physicians may not rely on *(1) conversations which have not been documented or (2) on standardized hospital consent forms.*

However, there are several measures physicians may take which will be quite effective in a court of law. For those procedures which a physician repeatedly performs, it may be practical and useful to develop carefully prepared written explanations, in lay language, which spell out the risks and alternative methods of treatment. The patient could be asked to read the form in advance and then be given the opportunity to discuss it with his physician before consent is requested. Other methods of conveying the information should be explored. In certain settings, it may be practical to reduce the explanations to tape and play the recording for the patient.

Q: **From the physician's point of view, is there more to it than the imparting of this information?**

A: Regardless of whether the physician relies on a conversation, written material, or a tape recording, *it is essential that the physician personally discuss the matter with the patient and make detailed notes of the discussion and the patient's reactions in the patient's medical chart.* These notes should be made at the time of the discussion or as soon thereafter as is physically possible to make the entries. A physician's entries in the patient's medical chart are his best protection in the event of a lawsuit.

Q: **Can my office staff assist me in fulfilling the obligations of informed consent?**

A: The Supreme Court made it crystal clear that the duty to inform and explain rests with the physician *and the physician alone.* Physicians should no more delegate this duty to a nurse, admission clerk, receptionist, or any other nonphysician than they would delegate the performance of major surgery to such persons. Legal protection flows from the physician (1) doing it himself and (2) recording what he does in the patient's chart or record.

on the matter of informed consent
for California orthopaedic surgeons

The Advisory Panel for Orthopaedic Surgeons of the California Medical Association has met and studied the problems of informed consent with particular reference to the recent California Supreme Court decision of *Cobbs v. Grant*.

This landmark decision imposes on the physician a new and greatly expanded concept of what constitutes informed consent for medical and surgical treatment of patients. The wording of the decision was reviewed in detail with attorneys who represent the California Medical Association, and it is clear that the court demands that physicians inform patients of all significant risks or potential hazards of their care.

The decision also clearly indicates that the main factor in determining the adequacy of the physician's job in explaining or informing the patient would be based on an evaluation of the *communication* that occurred between the physician and the patient.

The advisory panel could not agree upon a single form or type of communication after exploring a variety of possible methods of informing patients. Areas that the panel discussed included narrative written forms explaining the multiple risks; check-off

Prepared by the California Medical Association's Scientific
Advisory Panel to the Specialty Section on Orthopaedics.

lists to be used as outlines for the physician in discussing risks; taped programs; audiovisual programs; as well as the Tel-Med type program available through some local medical societies.

The conclusions of the group were as follows:

1. Communication is the key to informed consent, and documentation of this is the essence of maximum protection from nuisance or unwarranted malpractice suits.

2. Written forms may be helpful, but if the physician does not discuss the problems brought out in the forms and record in his progress notes that he has done so, the written form may be not only inadequate as protection against unwarranted litigation but may be *harmful*.

3. The *most protection* can be obtained from a written entry in the doctor's progress notes, stating that he has explained the nature of the procedure to the patient, and given a balanced presentation of the possible benefits and specific risks to which the procedure exposes the patient, and the alternative methods of care available.

What is critical in the above suggestions is that the doctor document the discussion or conversation with the patient in his notes, indicating the patient's response, as well as indicating that he has covered essential problems that the patient must consider before giving his consent to both medical and surgical care.

The following document titled "Reality of Consent—Physician's Duty of Disclosure" is the instruction that a California trial court judge may give the jury when a malpractice case depends upon whether the physician gave the patient information adequate to obtain an informed consent before treatment. Any informed consent procedure carried out by the physician will be judged against this instruction to the jury, and it would be worthwhile for a physician to acquaint himself with this so that one may judge for himself the adequacy of the informed consent procedure that he presently uses.

BAJI 6.11 (1972 Revision)
Reality of Consent—Physician's Duty of Disclosure

It is the duty of a physician or surgeon to disclose to his patient all relevant information to enable the patient to make an informed decision regarding the proposed operation or treatment.

There is no duty to discuss minor risks inherent in common procedures when such procedures very seldom result in serious ill effects.

However, when a procedure inherently involves a known risk of death or serious bodily harm, it is the physician's or surgeon's duty to disclose to his patient the possibility of such outcome and to explain in lay terms the complications that might possibly occur. The physician or surgeon must also disclose such additional information as a skilled practitioner of good standing would provide under the same or similar circumstances.

(There is no duty to make disclosure of risks when the patient requests that he not be so informed or where the procedure is simple and the danger remote and commonly understood to be remote.)

(Also, a physician or surgeon has no duty of disclosure beyond that required of physicians and surgeons of good standing in the same or similar locality when he relied upon facts which would demonstrate to a reasonable man that the disclosure would so seriously upset the patient that the patient would not have been able to rationally weigh the risks of refusing to undergo the recommended (treatment) (operation).)

Notwithstanding the patient's consent to a proposed treatment or operation, failure of the physician or surgeon to inform the patient as stated in this instruction before obtaining such consent is negligence and renders the physician or surgeon subject to liability for any injury (proximately) (legally) resulting from the (treatment) (operation) if a reasonably prudent person in the patient's position would not have consented to the (treatment) (operation) if he had been adequately informed of all the significant perils.

Use Note

This instruction is designed for use following instruction 6.10 in cases in which the patient has consented to a certain operation or course of treatment but a potential complication results, the occurrence of which was not an integral part of the operation or treatment procedure but merely a known risk which was not disclosed to the patient before obtaining his consent.

Cobbs v. Grant, 8 Cal. 3d 229, 104 Cal. Rptr. 505, 502 P.2d 1.

The burden of going forward with evidence of nondisclosure rests on the plaintiff. Once such evidence has been produced, then the burden of going forward with evidence pertaining to justification for failure to disclose shifts to the physician. *Cobbs v. Grant, supra.*

Comment

Cobbs v. Grant, 8 Cal. 3d 229, 104 Cal. Rptr. 505, 502 P.2d 1.

appendix c

authorization for and consent to surgery or special diagnostic or therapeutic procedures (nonteaching hospitals)

To _____
Name of Patient

Your admitting physician is _____, M.D.

Your surgeon is _____, M.D.

1. The hospital maintains personnel and facilities to assist your physicians and surgeons in their performance of various surgical operations and other special diagnostic and therapeutic procedures. These surgical operations and special diagnostic or therapeutic procedures all may involve calculated risks of complications, injury, or even death, from both known and unknown causes and no warranty or guarantee has been made as to result or cure. Except in a case of emergency or exceptional circumstances, these operations and procedures are therefore not performed upon patients unless and until the patient has had an opportunity to discuss them with his physician. Each patient has the right to consent to or refuse any proposed operation or special procedure (based upon the description or explanation received).

2. Your physicians and surgeons have determined that the operations or special procedures listed below may be beneficial in the diagnosis or treatment of your condition. Upon your authorization and consent, such operations or special procedures will be performed for you by your physicians and surgeons and/or by other physicians and surgeons selected by them. The persons in attendance for the purpose of administering anesthesia or performing other specialized professional services, such as radiology, pathology, and the like, are not the agents, servants, or employees of the hospital or your physician or surgeon, but are independent contractors performing specialized services on your behalf and, as such, are your agents, servants, or employees. Any tissue or member severed in any operation will be disposed of in the discretion of the pathologist, except _____

3. Your signature opposite the operations or special procedures listed below constitutes your acknowledgment (i) that you have read and agreed to the foregoing, (ii) that the operations or special procedures have been adequately explained to you by your attending physicians or surgeons and that you have all of the information that you desire, and (iii) that you authorize and consent to the performance of the operations or special procedures.

Operation or Procedure	Date	Time

Signature_____
                              Patient
Signature_____
                              Witness

(If patient is a minor or unable to sign, complete the following): Patient is a minor, or is unable to sign, because _____

_____

_____	_____
Father	Guardian
_____	_____
Mother	Other Person and Relationship

authorities cited

Cases

Aiken v. Clary, Missouri, p. 27

Bang v. Charles T. Miller Hospital, Minnesota, p. 23

Berkey v. Anderson, California, p. 23

Bing v. Thunig, New York, p. 20

Block v. McVay, South Dakota, p. 37

Bly v. Rhoads, Virginia, p. 27

Bowers v. Talmage, Florida, pp. 26, 30

Butler v. Berkeley, North Carolina, pp. 27, 33

Canterbury v. Spence, District of Columbia, pp. 28-34, 37-38, 40

Cathemer v. Hunter, Arizona, pp. 24, 47

Cobbs v. Grant, California, pp. 21, 24, 26, 29-31, 34, 37-40, 62-63, 65, 67-69, 71-77

Congrove v. Holmes, Ohio, p. 32

Cooper v. Roberts, Pennsylvania, pp. 23, 28, 32, 34

DiFilippo v. Preston, Delaware, p. 27

Ditlow v. Kaplan, Florida, p. 27

Downer v. Veilleux, Maine, pp. 23, 26, 34

Ferrara v. Galluchio, New York, p. 39

Ficklin v. Macfarlane, Utah, p. 27

Fiorentino v. Wenger, New York, pp. 19, 29

Note: Additional authorities not cited in the text may be obtained from the American Medical Association by addressing a request for bibliographies entitled *Cases on Informed Consent* and *Law of Informed Consent* both published in February 1974, to Office of the General Counsel, American Medical Association, 535 N. Dearborn St., Chicago, IL 60610.

Schloendorff v. Society of New York Hospitals, New York,
   pp. 20, 24
Schroeder v. Lawrence, Massachusetts, p. 35
Scott v. Wilson, Texas, p. 30
Shack v. Holland, New York, p. 19
Shetter v. Rochelle, Arizona, pp. 33-34
Small v. Gifford Memorial Hospital, Vermont, pp. 32, 34
Starnes v. Taylor, North Carolina, p. 30
Stauffer v. Karabin, Colorado, p. 27
Stottlemire v. Cawood, District of Columbia, p. 30
Terry v. Albany Medical Center Hospital, New York, p. 24
Trogun v. Fruchtman, Wisconsin, pp. 26, 34, 37, 40
Watson v. Clutts, North Carolina, p. 38
Wilkinson v. Vesey, Rhode Island, pp. 24, 26, 28, 30, 32, 34-35,
   37-39
Williams v. Menehan, Kansas, pp. 29, 39
Wilson v. Scott, Texas, p. 27
Yeates v. Harms, Kansas, p. 30
Young v. Yarn, Georgia, p. 20
ZeBarth v. Swedish Hospital Medical Center, Washington, p. 27
Zeleznik v. Jewish Chronic Disease Hospital, New York, p. 32

Law Reviews

A Doctor's Duty to Inform—Holland v. Sisters of Saint Joseph
of Peace, *Utah L. Rev.*, pp. 23, 37
A Reappraisal of Liability for Unauthorized Medical Treatment,
Minn. L. Rev., p. 22
An Analysis of "Informed Consent," *Fordham L. Rev.*, pp. 21, 37
Informed Consent: A New Standard for Texas, *St. Mary's L. J.*,
pp. 28, 32
Informed Consent: Looking for the Action, *U. Ill. L. Forum*,
pp. 23, 25-26
Informed Consent and the Danger of Bias in the Formation of
Medical Disclosure Practices, *Wis. L. Rev.*, pp. 23, 28
Informed Consent in Kentucky after the Medical Malpractice
Insurance and Claims Act of 1976, *Ky. L. J.*, p. 28
Informed Consent Liability, *Drake L. Rev.*, pp. 23, 33, 36

Informed Consent to Therapy, *Nw. U. L. Rev.*, p. 30
New Trends in Informed Consent? *Neb. L. Rev.*, pp. 21, 33
The Expansion of Liability for Medical Accidents:
From Negligence to Strict Liability by Way of Informed Consent,
Neb. L. Rev., pp. 29, 33, 36, 38-39

Statutes

Alaska Stat., pp. 41, 45, 53-54
Ariz. Rev. Stat., p. 47
Ark. Stat., pp. 50-51
Colo. Rev. Stat., pp. 48-49, 56-57
Del. Code Ann., pp. 41, 44-45, 47-48, 51-52, 54
Fla. Stat., pp. 41, 46, 48, 52-55
Ga. Code Ann., pp. 50-51
Haw. Sess. Laws Act, 1976, pp. 41, 53
Idaho Code, pp. 41, 44, 50, 62, 64
Iowa Code Ann., pp. 41, 43
Ky. Rev. Stat. Ann., pp. 24, 41, 51, 53
La. Stat. Ann., pp. 41, 44, 50-51
Me. Rev. Stat., pp. 41, 46, 49-50
Miss. Code of 1972, pp. 50-51
Mo. Stat. Ann., pp. 50-51
Neb. Rev. Stat., pp. 41, 45
Nev. Rev. Stat., pp. 41, 44, 51-52, 55-56
N.H. Laws, 1977, p. 41
N.Y. Civ. Prac. Law and Rules (McKinney Supp. 1976), p. 55
N.Y. Pub. Health Laws (McKinney Supp. 1976), pp. 41, 42, 46,
    51-52, 54
N.C. Gen. Stat., pp. 41, 46, 49-50, 52-53
Ohio Rev. Code Ann., pp. 41, 43-44, 52, 56-57
Or. Laws, p. 41
Pa. Stat. Ann., pp. 41, 51, 54
R.I. Gen. Laws, pp. 41, 56
Tenn. Code Ann., pp. 41, 45-46, 55
Tex. Sess. Law Serv., 1977, pp. 41, 46-48, 51-52, 57
Utah Code Ann., pp. 42, 46, 54
Vt. Stat. Ann., pp. 42, 45, 49, 53-55
Washington Rev. Code Ann., pp. 42, 46, 48, 51, 55, 62-63

References

All-Industry Committee Special Malpractice Review: 1974 Closed Claim Survey, *Insurance Services Office,* p. 6

Annotation, 52 A.L.R. 3d 1054, p. 27

Controversy, Alternatives, and Decisions in Complying with the Legal Doctrine of Informed Consent, *Radiology,* p. 37

FDA Regulations, 21 CFR, Part 310; HEW Regulations, 45 CFR, Part 46, p. 10

"How Lawyers Handle Medical Malpractice Cases: An Analysis of the Important Medicolegal Study," *DHEW,* p. 23

JCAH Accreditation Manual for Hospitals, February 1978 edition, pp. 14-15

Medical Malpractice, *D. Louisell and H. Williams,* p. 24

The Patient's Bill of Rights, AHA statement, pp. 1, 5-7, 10, 15

Handbook of the Law of Torts, 4th edition, 1971, *W. L. Prosser,* pp. 19, 25

1977 Report of the Commission on Medical Professional Liability, *American Bar Association,* p. 7

Report of the Secretary's Commission on Medical Malpractice, *DHEW Publication No. (OS) 73-88,* p. 7

Trustee, Oct. 1977, p. 1

Some Advice on "Informed Consent," *California Medical Association,* pp. 71-77

On the Matter of Informed Consent for California Orthopaedic Surgeons, California Medical Association, pp. 79-82

Authorization for and consent to surgery or special diagnostic or therapeutic procedures (nonteaching hospitals), California Medical Association, pp. 83-84